Side-Steps

Side-Steps

a rugby diary, 1984/85

Gerald Davies

and

John Morgan

HODDER AND STOUGHTON
LONDON SYDNEY AUCKLAND TORONTO

British Library Cataloguing in Publication Data
Davies, Gerald, *1945–*
    Sidesteps: a rugby diary, 1985.
    1. Rugby football – History – 20th century
    I. Title   II. Morgan, John, *1929–*
    796.33'3'09048   GV944.85

    ISBN 0-340-38113-2

For Cilla and Mary
who, since they do not
watch rugby, may not
read beyond this page

Contents

Illustrations

CREDITS

1 Gren cartoon by courtesy of the *South Wales Echo*
2 Aled Morgan
3 Dennis Stephens
4 Colorsport
5 Allsport

Foreword

What follows is not a formal account of a season in rugby football. The book's title, unlike so many International selections in the past year, has been chosen very carefully. We have had two aims. One is to interpret what happened on the field of play, concentrating on elements which would not be the concern of someone giving a match report for the next day's newspaper reader. (The results of some key matches are given in the appendices.) Impressionism has been the ambition rather than detail. A game is much more than its result, however heretical that sentiment might seem to the engaged player or spectator. Thus TGRD side-steps through the field of play.

The second aim, which involves JM moving from foot to foot through clubs of high and low degree, has been to express the social character of rugby's believers. To look at rugby in this way is really to look at British life in a patch of turf, even to detect a metaphor for the society's condition. Also, happily, it is a means of discovering the humour and affection mutually displayed in what may, to the indifferent, look a rough pastime. The opening and concluding chapters take the form of a chat about these matters.

In building up our diary for the season we have been helped in our travels throughout Britain, France and the Far East by HTV Wales to whom we express our gratitude. We are especially thankful to Don Llewelyn, the director of a film on the same subject as this book, and should also like to thank *The Times* and the *Western Mail* for whom we have been writing this season for their kind permission to reproduce the spirit, if not the text, of some observations. To name all those men and women in scores of rugby clubs who have given us their time and hospitality, would take a chapter in itself. They know who they are and should they read this, we would like to thank them for their generosity. If *Side-Steps* has a theme it is that fun has lately been too much absent from rugby football at its highest – not its lowest – level. We hope we can communicate our pleasure and that this may persuade some in power to ask themselves whether it is not time that we saw some changes made.

TGRD
Coed y Paen, Gwent

JM
Mork, Glos

1

The Nature of the Game

> . . . and we'll talk with them too,
> Who loses, who wins, who's in, who's out;
> And take upon's the mystery of things.
>
> Shakespeare, *King Lear*

TGRD Why do you take up sport in the first place? Because you enjoy playing. That's my basic premise. As a schoolboy or a child you play because it is a fundamental enjoyment. If you enjoy rugby, then you take it up. You also find, perhaps, that if you have some skill in that sport you want to keep playing it. Another influence is the community, the environment. In Wales of course this leads you to rugby and being in a team gives a young person a sense of identity with a group. It's worth remembering this because as you grow up you tend to forget those simple things. You get involved in competition and coaching and it is important for the club to win, and you tend to forget those elements that first started you off in the game. I do think it is important for players to remember that basically you still take part because you enjoy it.

JM When I was young, I enjoyed playing rugby very much and I played in the school team. But there came a point when I realised that, while I was enjoying it, I was never really going to be a player of the highest class and this could well be because I wasn't good enough; but it was also because I wouldn't put the effort into keeping fit or training or taking part to the degree that someone like yourself did. So while I might have started off with the same spirit as yourself, there does come a point where

11

the mediocre player drops out. What was it that made you determined to go on playing for so long at such a high level?

TGRD   What persuades a person to keep on playing and separates him from the rest who don't is mental, the psychological motivating factor peculiar to him. It's the vital ingredient which every talented player needs to have if he is to achieve his potential. Many players drop by the wayside because they haven't the tenacity, the nous, the inspiration or the motivation to want to go on. I remember my own earliest inspiration. There was a young boy in our village who won an Under 15 Welsh Schoolboy cap and brought his jersey and cap back to the village to be admired. And I wanted to emulate that. I failed to do it at Under 15, I managed it at Under 18. Then it got into my blood. Having achieved one thing, you want to go to the next, like getting a senior cap for Wales. Having got that first one, you don't want to be a one-cap wonder, the fate of so many, and by the time you have got several caps then it has become an addiction. There are several points during your career when you think about giving up, perhaps because of the pressure, because it is time consuming; perhaps you wonder whether all this effort in an amateur game is worthwhile. But in Wales the standing a Welsh player has in the community is a very seductive thing. And you thrill to the roar of the crowd.

JM   Is the roar of the crowd very potent at the Arms Park? Does it deafen you?

TGRD   You are only aware of it when the game is at a stop. When the game is in flow you are very rarely aware of the noise because you are concentrating on lots of other things, but you are aware that you are playing on your own patch and that everyone is there to support you. The crowd is an important element. There is a difference between playing in front of one man and a dog and playing in front of 60,000 people. Some say that this is an enormous pressure for players to bear, but it's a pressure that International players of the right calibre revel in. Jean-Pierre Rives has described it as the special ingredient. You come back for more.

JM Do you feel that you are bound to be playing better because that crowd is there?

TGRD Yes, it certainly gets the adrenalin going. For the first dozen or so games the only impression you get is of things happening very quickly. You can't remember details of games, just an overall impression, and before you know it, the game is over and done with. The longer you go on playing, the more you become aware of what is happening, and the more enjoyable the whole experience becomes.

JM So there is pleasure. If you write something that is satisfying and feel you have said what you wanted to say in an elegant manner, I think I understand that pleasure. So when you were in such a great team for so long, did you have a positive sense of aesthetic delight that you were with such gifted people?

TGRD I remember after I had got about a dozen caps a certain sense of dissatisfaction and even disappointment set in. I wondered was it worth it. The Welsh team wasn't performing all that well, we won a few games and lost a few. There was no sense of continuity, of knowing quite what we were up to. But then coaching came in and Clive Rowlands arrived and he, more than anyone, gave an identity to the Welsh team. Success came. And the success bred more success. At a crucial period this persuaded me to hang on. Not only was it a good thing in

13

itself, but I was in the company of good men, of friends. We won the Triple Crown three times in a row and this captured the public imagination in a way that I had not known before, and that too was a driving force.

JM   As a spectator in that period, I had the sense that people like yourself, Barry John, Gareth Edwards, Mervyn Davies and John Taylor, were playing International rugby yet looking as if you were enjoying yourselves. Did you have a sense then that you were enjoying it, and that there was almost an artistic, as well as a physical pleasure in being with people like that – men who were playing rugby of such quality that it was an extra element in the game?

TGRD   Enjoyment was always important because that is the bottom line. Unless there is that element of enjoyment, I don't care how good a team you are or how competitive, if you lose that sense of enjoyment then rugby is not worth the candle. I think what has happened over the last few years is that the game has become more and more competitive, people have become more and more analytical about it, and coaching has tried to impose a certain way of playing without appreciating that in the end it is a matter of enjoyment. You got pleasure out of being in a good team and that gives a shared experience and enjoyment. But there is also within the team, as we played then, the player's contribution, which is something independent of the others, the self-satisfying kind of pleasure in knowing that you have performed well and that you were being allowed the opportunity to perform well. The wing can be a very isolated position, and if he doesn't feel as if he is contributing, then there can't be much enjoyment for him, however many times his team wins. Unless the individual player feels he has contributed to that win, he remains unfulfilled and empty.

JM   I suppose the triumph you had with the British
Lions in 1971 in New Zealand is regarded as the greatest
achievement of any British team abroad. Was the actual
touring fun? Or is the game such a preoccupation for the
player that he doesn't really know he's travelling?

TGRD   No, we enjoyed the travelling, visiting places,
meeting all sorts of people, going out to restaurants and
so on. In Bleddyn Williams' day of course the Lions were
away for six months of the year and two of those would
be spent on board ship. Today things have tended to
become a bit less leisurely and more intense, with the
number of games played cut down as well. But rugby is
still an amateur game and the great perk, for want of a
better word, is the travelling, a broadening of the hori-
zons which rugby football has given us. Of course there
is the other side of the coin. There are those moments
before a Test when you have a sense of fear. There are
just the thirty of you, alone in a foreign and distant
country, and the tension and pressure are at a peak. You
begin to wonder what on earth you are doing there.
There must be far more pleasurable things to be doing at
the height of summer back home.

JM   Was it much fun playing, then? Did you actually
enjoy being on the field?

TGRD   No question about it, yes I did. Back in '71 there
was such a marvellous atmosphere in the team due to
people like Carwyn James, John Dawes and Doug Smith.
A game is not just a physical confrontation, it's a matter
of techniques and skill, and also of attitudes. Attitudes
coming from the top and from within the team. If the
coach has a generous spirit which is able to instil a kind of
fun in the players, that makes for a better game on the
field than if he is tense and dour and oppressive. The
crucial point about 1971 in New Zealand was that there

was a great sense of fun and adventure. When you think of the players, you could never attribute adjectives like 'dour' or 'grim' or 'intense' to someone like Barry John or David Duckham or Willy John McBride. But though we had fun, there was also the common purpose, that serious objective which everyone wanted to achieve.

Coming back to the present, look at Mick Doyle of Ireland, he is a coach with a light-hearted, very laid back approach to things. He actually smiles quite frequently and I think, whilst Ireland were never the greatest team in the world, the psychological make up of that team was good enough to win the Championship this year because there was a kind of generosity about the way they approached the game.

JM   Reading about the 1971 tour or any of the great matches, there is a tendency afterwards for people to analyse it as if it were all preplanned. You can look at the game as a rather incoherent mess with people just running around and it all seems pure chance. Nowadays people don't look at a match like that, as one did when young. They tend instead to consider it much more as something that has been preordained by the coach. The players are under instruction and carrying out orders. At International level do you play with both a very strategic and a strong tactical sense, or is it much more arbitrary?

TGRD   In a game with a ball the shape it is, it can't be other than arbitrary a lot of the time. But what you are hinting at highlights some of what is going wrong at the moment. Coaches feel they can plan a game. There is no way that you can plan a game. There are so many variables: the weather, obscure laws which a fallible referee has to interpret, the players themselves, and the scope of their individual abilities. These days we all subscribe to the ideal of playing expansive fifteen-man

16

rugby. But you can't play like that all the time. You have to achieve what you can with the players you have facing the opposition you have. The pattern of play can't be dictated before kick-off. To distinguish between strategy and tactics: strategy is something you determine in a general sense before the game starts; tactics is what happens on the park. The cleverness of the players in the 'seventies was that there was sufficient confidence in the player in each position to determine the tactics as the game evolved. Gareth Edwards or Barry John or Phil Bennett would know when the ball should be moved or when it should be kicked.

JM   Barry used to tell me that he would look at you out on the wing and if he thought you were looking a bit cold, he'd let you have the ball!

TGRD   That's typical of his lovely arrogance – the majestic arrogance of the outside-half.

JM   But seriously, in that period it used to strike me as an observer that the backs didn't get all that much of the ball; that what happened was people like you or Barry or Gareth or Phil or JPR would frequently make something out of practically nothing. The moments which were decisive were very often the unexpected moments of individual brilliance. The excitement was in never knowing what was going to happen next.
   Having said that, this season International teams seem to have exhibited an almost spectacular stupidity. When we saw the Australians play Wales, for example, the visitors played a very intelligent game. They had very good forwards and they had the ball and knew what to do with it. Scotland and England played Australia subsequently, and they must have seen the Welsh match and what happened. Yet when Australia played Scotland, Scotland went and committed all the mistakes

17

Wales had made. Surely someone in Scotland must have said we mustn't play like this against the Australians because we have seen what they did to Wales. Yet they still went out at Murrayfield and played into the Wallabies' hands as if mesmerised. Surely that is not an example of the bad side of coaching so much as a failure of intelligence?

TGRD Yes, and there aren't that many clever people around at the moment. You do need to analyse the play of your opponents, and these days the coach has taken too much responsibility for this on himself. But when it comes to the sharp end, the most important person is of course the captain, because he is the one on the field. It's the captain who can encourage and instil those qualities needed to beat the opposition. You can have a broad strategy, which the coach ought to have analysed somewhere along the line, but it is the captain and the players on the field who determine how to win the game.

JM When you played for Wales and the British Lions John Dawes was captain for a long period, and then there was Mervyn Davies. How does the captain on the field actually express his analysis to his team? Does he come over and say, look, we have to change our tactics here, boys? If he were a centre, would he go and tell the forwards they must do something different?

TGRD Almost certainly. There is a kind of dialogue. There's always a great deal of chatter among the forwards anyway about who should be doing what. But the key position is always at half-back. It's at half-back the pattern of the game is determined, regardless of where the captain is. I was fortunate to play at a time when Wales and the Lions were particularly strong in those positions. The captain didn't have much to say to them because the halves knew what to do and when to do it.

This year Wales failed miserably to change tactics against Ireland at a crucial period in the last twenty minutes. The idea that Wales should persist in running the ball when they were being knocked down in mid-field shows a lack of awareness at half-back. Running and playing a lovely expansive game is just one kind of tactic. But if you want to win, it may during the course of the game be necessary to vary the tactic; you may have to adopt, for the sake of argument, the Pontypool approach for a while in order to wear the other team down or show up their weaknesses.

JM   Rugby of all games strikes me as being a team game. In rugby nobody can play well unless the team is playing well.

TGRD   Certainly, the players are cogs in the machine of the whole team. But those cogs have their own hierarchy. While the prop forward may plough his lonely furrow, the outside-half is a princely figure who cannot possibly be considered on the same plane. His personality has to be different, as indeed does the full-back's or the wing's. A clever coach like Carwyn James recognises these distinctions of personality and plays to individual strengths for the benefit of the team as a whole.

One of the perverse charms of rugby football is that the laws are so complicated the game is not clear cut in any way at all. Why does the scrum collapse? Whose fault is it? Why has a penalty been given? Why was it a free kick and not a penalty? What happens in the line-out? Was it a try under that great heap? Breweries have made their fortunes on post-match postmortems. The game gorges itself on all the talk.

JM   Are you suggesting then that rugby players must be cleverer than other sportsmen because they need to master such complicated laws?

TGRD   Far from it. I don't think many players know the laws. For my own part, I never actually read the rule book until very late in my life and that was only because I was captain of Cardiff and had to be sure of my ground if there was a point of disagreement with the referee. You have to have a legal mind to understand the laws. How many teams are there in Wales? About 900. How many of the players in those teams have actually read the laws? It must be a minuscule figure.

JM   So how will we all be interpreting the law when we have the promised World Cup in 1987? Will the players know the rules by then?

TGRD   I'd hate to guess. But I'm sure one trend now the World Cup has been inaugurated will be for individual nations to travel overseas more under their own flags and this will make the Lions less meaningful and probably get rid of them in the end.

JM   When we were down in the South of France looking at French rugby – and it was an entertaining and instructive trip – we had a very strong sense of the foreignness of the place. I wonder if more British clubs ought not to go and play more in Europe. They could afford to go more often to Holland or France than to New Zealand or Australia, after all. We have also heard on our travels about various players from Britain and the southern hemisphere who are now playing for French or Italian clubs and enjoying themselves immensely, and no doubt being rewarded. Should there be more of that?

TGRD   Yes, if I have any regrets, and I don't like to look over the shoulder at what might have been, but I would have loved to have had the opportunity to play in France for a year, not only to get to grips with French rugby, but to learn the language. As you say, Australians do it, New

Zealanders do it, some people from England have been doing it in recent years and I think it would be a good thing for Welsh rugby if players were able occasionally to move away from the Welsh environment, even if they only go to play for a while in Scotland or England. Welsh rugby has become very insular, and as a result we tend to become a little neurotic about it. We are not expansive enough in going out and meeting other people.

JM   I wonder if one reason they won't go is that if they are aspiring to play for their country they feel it's important to be under the eyes of the selectors at home: that home is where the cap is.

TGRD   That may very well be true. After all, one Welsh player this year decided to go on a two-week skiing holiday during the season and wasn't picked for the squad. But he captained the Welsh team in the end! I think, however, it is the language barrier more than anything that deters players from this exciting gamble.

JM   In the South of France it was clear that there were opportunities for young British players to have a very nice life and play a good class of rugby, and live in some style. It was a revelation to me and I don't think our young players are aware of what would be available to them. French players are certainly given preferential treatment, almost film-star status in the community. They are found jobs, flats, motor cars. You probably weren't aware of the fact but talking to the players in clubs and bars there, they could not believe you were not a millionaire. Because you were who you were and such a celebrated figure, they took it for granted that you, like so many French players we won't name, would be enormously rich. You would have a mansion and people would be coming to your house as a shrine, that kind of thing. It was a shock to them that you actually still need to work for a living!

TGRD   We are coming round to the whole prickly question of amateur status now. My belief is that the game ought to remain amateur but that the regulations should be redefined in the simplest possible terms. Players ought not to be paid for playing the game. There are very many good reasons for this, not least that I think the players themselves enjoy the game as it is without the enormous pressures footballers have because their livelihoods depend on footballing success and they live in fear of failure. Another reason why I think it should remain amateur is that the laws are much too complicated! The best professional sports are games like snooker or golf, which are non-contact and everyone knows precisely what is happening. But rugby football is not like that. Since each man has his price, who is to say what dirty deed might not be committed at the bottom of a ruck for the sake of pieces of silver?

What need changing however are the laws of amateurism, enshrined in twelve pages in the law book. Why can't a player write a book and get some money for it? Why can't he sponsor something? It's these peripheral matters that need sorting out to give players the benefit. After all, the Unions rake in enormous sums in sponsorship for International and Cup matches, and lots of money is ploughed into the game. But this doesn't make much sense to the man who plays week in, week out, at club level, and the Unions just don't realise that their money-making emphasis encourages similar ideas in the players.

When I was out in Hong Kong recently I spoke to Alan Jones, the very perceptive and articulate Australian coach, and he said what the players want is to be made to feel special. A sour note has been allowed to creep into our game because the Unions have shown a lack of generosity towards players. As Alan Jones said, why couldn't someone like Gould, their full-back, bring in some friends to the hotel and buy them a meal to thank them for their hospitality? The reason at the time was because he couldn't afford to do it. Why can't money be made available for something like that, or for entertaining wives or girl friends?

I can remember when I was captaining the Barbarians against the Lions at Twickenham in the royal Jubilee year, Jean-Pierre Rives wanted to have a bottle of wine with his dinner. But the four Home Unions had allowed us a cask of beer, so he was told to drink that. Well, beer is not the beverage your good Frenchman is accustomed to drink with a meal, especially when he's travelled from France to play in a gala game. But we had to work quite hard to get that one bottle of wine for Jean-Pierre Rives. And there were the Home Unions proudly boasting of how much they were giving to the Jubilee Trust that year. Profit came first, instead of the players' welfare.

JM   Looking at the English team and talking to English rugby folk during the season, I have the feeling the players themselves were so uncertain about being selected, were so insecure about their futures, that they looked unhappy on the field and couldn't give of their best.

TGRD   That could be said to apply to the Welsh, too, this year. I have spoken to players who have said that they dare not open their mouths to make a suggestion for fear they may not find themselves around for the next game. That is a very unhealthy situation because the whole point about rugby is that it should be a team experience, not just for the fifteen players, but for those who select and coach them to pool their talents.

JM   In England what struck me as odd was that there are players who are very good but have no interest in playing for England. They would rather play for their clubs, even small ones, than go and play for a big club and win an International cap. Now up until recently that seemed very unWelsh.

TGRD   Yes, the curious development in Welsh rugby – the players who do not want to continue to play for Wales.

JM   It can't have happened before, can it? Not so pointedly, I mean, people saying I am not playing for Wales again?

TGRD   It must be a symptom of what is going wrong at the moment.

JM   But we spectators tend to think that those chaps who are great players are not actually touched by human emotions on the field. It can be very difficult for people who haven't played in front of big crowds or to a high standard to understand what is necessarily going on in the mind of the player. Is he nervous? Is he thinking that he has just made a mistake? If he's a full-back is he worrying about the wind blowing too strongly in his face? Is his old knee injury playing up? Nowadays, when you see a recording of yourself in a match, which is such a furious and excitable affair, do you remember the try just like it was?

TGRD   As far as individual games are concerned, I have only a general memory of what actually happened in each. I don't think I have the kind of mind to remember the details. Though someone like Mike Gibson could remember the actual minutiae of a game and talk you through particular incidents.

JM   Let's consider some tries where you side-stepped past people or went for the corner and it didn't look as if you would make it. In your mind at the time, was there a blind determination; or did you have a scheme for out-witting people? Or was it done out of instinct?

TGRD   Largely out of instinct. From my point of view the worst thing that could happen to me was to have a lot of time to think about something on the rugby field. I'm sure this is true for most players. With regard to my side-step, if you are in a very enclosed space, with lots of bodies around, you act instinctively. But there were occasions when perhaps I had fifteen or twenty yards to my next opponent. Then I had time to think about it and that did make me just a little bit nervous. However, I always feel the man with the ball holds the advantage and it's the other person who has to react. So it's a case of getting him into a situation where he has no time for second thoughts and is inescapably committed.

JM   And if you were in a defensive position, was that instinctive as well?

TGRD   No, in defence you have to think more about the other player – what would I be doing in that situation if I had the ball? You have to try and cut down the number of options for your opponent. You can veer him out to the touchline, or suggest by your own positioning that he ought to come back inside. You have to channel him to do what *you* want him to do. I can remember in the Second Test in New Zealand in 1971 facing up to Brian Williams, a very formidable opponent and a lovely winger with speed and side-step, and a hefty fellow, too. He made about twenty yards on me in open field which really ought to put the defensive man in an awkward position. But I thought of the number of options he had open to him, and at the back of my mind I thought of the

New Zealand attitude. Knowing that he was much larger than I was, I guessed that Williams would have been told, "Run up to him and run over him." And that's precisely what he tried to do. He simply ran straight at me and I thought, well, that's not good thinking when he has all his other options open.

JM   So you were able to stop him?

TGRD   So I stopped him, that's right. I just stood in his way and he trampled all over me. But he didn't get very far because the pack caught up with him.

JM   In the days when I played rugby, I never used to think that it was a peculiarly rough game or a dirty game, or even a particularly tough game. But today, viewing the game as a spectator, there looks to be a pugilistic element in it. Why does it look so much rougher now than it was to experience? Did you use to think to yourself, what am I doing here with all these other fellows punching each other and kicking each other and trying to hit me? What a daft way of endangering oneself, and for what?

TGRD   That is the great mystery. There was never a stage when I thought rugby was so rough a game that I didn't want to be part of it. Certainly there were odd things going on in the scrum, but I never thought it was a dirty game. I was caught at the bottom of a ruck or a maul sometimes, but there were only one or two instances in my whole career when anything untoward happened. Whether that was because there was some sort of gentle-manly understanding that forwards don't touch the backs, I rather doubt. But you're right, now I've stopped playing and started watching, it certainly does look rougher and tougher and more violent from the touch-line.

26

JM   I broke a shoulder, a collar bone, a thumb and four ribs playing rugby. The four ribs were due to having a game in the Midlands for a team where the scrum-half was clearly demented. I was playing at outside-half and he kept on giving me the ball with about four blokes at the same time. That would never happen in Welsh rugby. But all that's a different thing from calculated violence and over-combative play. Should the authorities be dealing more firmly with that?

TGRD   Well, they do have a policy to a certain extent already, but it isn't followed through in as convincing a manner as it ought to be. If a player is sent off the field, he won't be open for selection for the national team. There are a very few thugs around the rugby clubs who can make the game disreputable. Generally speaking players keep to the laws. Speaking now as a back talking about forwards, I think the unspoken agreement that the forwards can get on with whatever they like and that punches are okay is wrong. In fact the thugs tend to use other means of expressing themselves, like studs and going for the eyes and the mouth and the nose. Though there are very few of those around, they do bring the game into disrepute.

JM   So what, then, do you feel is the peculiar appeal of the game?

TGRD   I loved playing it and I still love watching it. One of its unique qualities is the variety of people it gives a chance to. There are very few other outdoor ball games a chap the size and weight of a prop forward could play to a high level. I love the way it caters for all shapes and sizes from the lanky second row to the tiny winger, no bigger than a bar of soap. And then there's the social aspect which is a binding factor that brings people back every Saturday to play because they are with a bunch of friends. There's an eighty-minute period when they play, they combat the other team, which gives them a sense of identity, and at the end of the day both sides can still come together to socialise in the club house, and that is the binding factor of rugby.

JM   I suppose the fact the game is spreading through the world so fast now must mean that its appeal is great?

TGRD   It is very popular and I think this World Cup the International Board are arranging for 1987 is going to be a crucial watershed in the game's development. It could be a spectacle or it could be deadly boring because of the way the game is arranged and the laws are written. That kind of showpiece is a delicate balance between enjoyment and winning.

JM   It's a long time since I played rugby. I have been watching now for decades, but I still recall playing and the excitement of it, even dreadful player that I was. But for you it must be more poignant now when you go to a match and watch Wales play. Do you find the experience of sitting there and *not* playing a saddening one? Does it make you melancholy that the years have gone and you are no longer on the fields of praise?

TGRD   No, and I don't have any sense of envy either. You know my philosophy. I don't keep looking over my shoulder. Having experienced successes and failures, wins and losses, you realise both are important. But in the end what is nice, of course, is to look back on a period of success. However, that period of my life is over now and, looking at the game today, I would just like the present players to experience what we experienced.

JM   But it wasn't just the success or the victory, was it? It was success in style?

28

TGRD   Style, yes. There was a lot of fun. The rugby player can train as much as he likes during the week, but his reward is to go out there and play and try to put into practice those things he has been taught. The coach can't do that. The only satisfaction for the coach is in winning. If the team doesn't win, the coach is dissatisfied. But for the player, win or lose, at least he has been out there trying to do something. That's the paradox – the curious blend of joy and achievement. Because there should be fun in the game. If there is no fun in rugby football, there is no game.

2

September

Pontypool! thou dirtiest of dirty places . . .
Yet thou dost show to us wonderous phrases.
Richard Hall (1817–66)

1 September

TGRD It is inevitable. Not only at the start of a new season when there is a pinching excitement in the air at odds with the ripening fullness of the year, but also at intervals later, when the air is much sharper and less inviting, when a particular match transmits an intoxicating energy of its own, like Cardiff v. Pontypool, or Llanelli playing London Welsh on Boxing Day, the teasing question is asked: "Shouldn't you be out there?"

Even eight years after the boots have been safely tucked away, someone, somewhere, is impelled to enquire or to nudge away the years for his or my benefit, as if to warm up a recollection long left in cold storage.

"Don't you wish that you were out there again?" "*Do* you miss it?" "We could do with you today."

It is a kind of compliment to which I reply "Thank you", for the memories – mine and, I hope, his. It is a warm massage to be reminded. Since I stopped playing I have heard people express such generous memories about my playing era, sentiments of which I was quite genuinely unaware at the time, because when you are playing the public erects a sort of invisible screen around you, to preserve the species perhaps, and only now has the barrier been raised. Then things never quite got said in the same way.

"Do you miss it?" It is not asked in all seriousness, but I do puzzle them, I think, when I say no, so emphatically. But at this time of year I have second thoughts. I should say, "Yes, I do miss it." But not for the reason they might have in mind. I miss the way the short summer months would once have done a good job in removing the staleness of the previous eight months of rugby. The prospect of a new season revives the appetite. I loved the game. And still do, thank goodness. There might be a yawning gap if I didn't. Age cannot wither the enthusiasm, nor custom stale the variety of what I see in rugby football. There is nothing quite like another rugby season. By the end I may very well be disappointed. Certainly I shall look forward to another summer break. But the anticipation, come September, is still there: the season in prospect.

Yet, for all that, I cannot now take the beginning of the season that seriously. Nor the end for that matter, when the game, apart from the Cup competitions, gradually meanders to a close with the Internationals over and studying form becomes almost meaningless. When I played I enjoyed it all, but that may be part of the difference between being a journalist and a player. In studying form the middle part of the season, December and January, is perhaps the vital period; for a player, it could be the bleakest. But there is nothing of importance at stake at the start. The players are limbering up, getting rid of the muscle cobwebs, getting tuned to the needs of the game and the depressing limits of flabby flesh. Rugby's a bit like a youthful posterior. The kind that gets appreciated has got to be tight and shapely. The early-season game is too loose to attract a second glance. Which is what happened at Rodney Parade where Newport beat Coventry 28-12, and where the long dry summer had left many a grassless patch.

TGRD   A week into the season and I wonder how the players will survive their clubs' absurdly overloaded fixture lists. Assuming that clubs who make early exits from the Cup competition will no doubt arrange other fixtures, all the clubs apart from Cardiff (47), Aberavon (48) and Llanelli (49) will play over fifty matches this season. Pontypridd, I see, has the dubious distinction of heading the table with fifty-five, closely followed by Ebbw Vale (54) and Bridgend (53) – twice as many as their New Zealand equivalents, the provincial sides. Unless the clubs spread the fixtures around among the players in their squads, this is an unreasonable number of games to play in any one season. It may be no bad thing to have a crowded first month or so, since the coaches can use these matches to determine who their best players are. But too many games blunt the edges of a fine player's skill.

Once the dark winter months come, there should be no mid-week games. Saturday should be reserved as the big match day. I learned that much a long time ago at London Welsh. You can tell the difference in the way players get changed in the dressing room. They do so eagerly when they really want to play, they go through the motions when they do not. After a day's work there was no doubt which category they fell into on a wet Wednesday night in December. It seemed too much like an extra shift. Overtime without pay. To play rugby should be a special occasion, something to look forward to. Nowadays there is a surfeit. Instead the clubs should whet the appetite; keep the supporters wanting more. And if that doesn't please the Treasurer, then I would suggest that fewer games would bring in a bigger crowd on Saturday. The players might have a spring in their step once more. Rugby is meant for Saturday afternoons.

These thoughts are prompted by talking to Neville Walsh, sometime lawyer and full-time manager of the Crawshay's Welsh XV. They have recently returned from France, delighted with the fact that they've just joined Auckland and the London Welsh as the only visitors to beat Béziers on their own ground since the French club came to prominence in the late 'sixties. During that time Béziers have dominated the French Championship, winning eleven times. As they are the current holders Crawshay's could be forgiven for feeling well satisfied in winning a superb match by 24-21, after which they were given a standing ovation by the 12,000 crowd.

Although Neville Walsh has since been congratulated for striking a blow for Welsh rugby and for strengthening Cambro/Gallic relations, the prospect of their visit was initially viewed with dismay by some Welsh officials. By playing before the season began and was properly under way the Crawshay's committee were said to be placing an additional burden and making unnecessary demands on the players' time.

However, rather than point an accusing finger at a travelling side who have a reputation for enjoyment both on and off the field, it would be far better if the clubs' attention were drawn to exercising a more stringent control over their domestic fixtures. It is a commonly, but mistakenly, held view that it is these representative fixtures, Crawshay's, the Welsh Academicals, even the Barbarians, that cause the pressure on present-day players. But it is these very matches that can often alleviate the pressure, as they release players from the treadmill of so many club games. No one should seriously condemn any player in these circumstances, particularly those in the upper echelons, for exercising his discretion to choose the games in which he appears. It is to be hoped that clubs will eventually see the sense of cutting down on their present punishing fixture lists in the best interest of the game as a whole. Saturdays only is quite enough.

Will the players in the Welsh team have as much fun as those with the Crawshay's?

8 September

TGRD   The season has begun quietly – no hullabaloo as in 1982 with the disclosures of alleged boot money, nor any controversy as in 1983 about David Lord's professional circus. Today it was announced that Andy Haden, the New Zealand lock, had been cleared by the New Zealand RFU council of breaching rugby's amateur regulations. He had had to face an eighteen-man council to answer charges that he had advanced and promoted professional rugby in his book *Boots 'n' All*. The incident highlighted once more the absurdity of these regulations and the desperate need to review them and to reconstruct the whole, Victorian edifice of amateur status.

12 September

TGRD   To see as many games as possible at the start of the season – to study form. Tonight it is Pontypool v. Newport. Once again it is important to have a look at David Bishop, in case something happens to Terry Holmes again this year, as it did last.

Bishop is a devastating player, as he showed in this game. He is a prolific try scorer, again he scored in this match. Last year he scored a post-war record number of thirty-nine tries for Pontypool and in total has accumulated seventy-six tries in seventy-seven games since joining the club from Ebbw Vale three years ago.

Against Newport tonight he was injured but remained on the field to play an influential role in the victory. He is a tough, tenacious player whom the opposition are rarely able to pin down, and when they do he pops up again like one of those toys with a round weighted base. His play is determinedly individualistic within Pontypool's often rigid pattern. It is his dominating personality that now, as once did the Pontypool front row, encapsulates the image of the club and which insists on perpetuating the nine-man game. With a slight change of emphasis it could be so different.

There is the story, no doubt apocryphal like so many that attach themselves to the legendary Ray Prosser, of the time he took a new recruit at scrum-half on a little inspection of the beautiful park at Pontypool.

"Here," he said, "on your own line, if the forwards give you the ball, you kick to touch." He then moved down the pitch. "And here," pointing to the 22-metre line, "if you get the ball you kick to that touch, right?" They moved to the half-way line. "Here, you've got the choice. You either kick it to touch or you kick it high to the middle of the field to their full-back, right?"

"But when do I pass the ball?" asked the puzzled player.

"Not until you get to this position," said the great man, pointing at the opposition 22-metre line. "Here you can pass the ball to the outside-half, and he can kick!"

But a team which accumulates 1,607 points, as Pontypool did last season, cannot rely solely for their survival on a pack of forwards and a half-back. On this particular Wednesday evening in the first half there were shades of brilliance in their team work and also some delicate touches – not a phrase that comes readily to mind at Pontypool Park – as they scored three marvellous tries. It was irresistible stuff and it all occurred when Bishop, handicapped with injury, was less sure of himself and quite happy to delegate much of the responsibility to others. For whatever reason his self-confidence returned in the second half and, with his selfish use of possession, the game died.

He inevitably scored a brilliant try, but it followed half a dozen attempts during which he consistently ignored

Goldsworthy the fly-half outside him. Those who make claims for him to understudy Holmes in the Welsh team ought to bear his approach in mind. Quality of decision is especially important at scrum-half. At present the flaw in Bishop's game is that others in the backs can only take part after he has exhausted all the possibilities open to him. That is an expense the Welsh team can ill afford.

19 September

JM   Sitting at the side of the swimming pool at Reid's Hotel in Madeira, far out in the warm Atlantic, I read a report of a match by Gerald in *The Times* and felt guilty enough to write him a letter. Or rather wrote him a letter because I was not enjoying myself, and might as well work. An episode on the trip to Madeira reminded me of a joke played by that wonderful half-back Onllwyn Brace when he was captain of the Oxford University team. He and his English colleague Peter Robbins persuaded a South African member of the team that he needed a passport to enter Wales for a match at Cardiff. Naturally, he didn't have his with him, so he was placed in the boot of the coach crossing the bridge at Chepstow: more, so was he on the journey home to Oxford.

The relevance of the tale, I wrote, defensively, was that I had succeeded in bringing into Madeira a friend, Siân Lloyd, who had lost her passport. At London Heathrow they had said her chances were not good, since Portugal, to which Madeira belongs, was not yet in the Common Market. At Madeira airport, once I had taken the wild gamble of bringing her along, they said she would have to be deported. It was unlikely Britain would allow her back in. There was I in Madeira safely: she could have turned out to be the Welsh feminine equivalent of the Flying Dutchman. I asked the Portuguese in Madeira if I could ring Lisbon. They properly said no. People without passports were not allowed into countries. I mentioned I was hoping to have a rest because I was writing a book about rugby this season. One had played at university. I dropped the names of a few Welsh players I knew. Such a transformation! My friend was allowed in. Not that I think she understood quite how difficult a transaction it had been. Some people are expected to be able to organise that kind of thing perhaps.

She doesn't play tennis either, and I don't swim: a steam hammer is at work the whole day building a hotel next door. I would have been better off watching Newport play Pontypool in the rain. Such was my message of encouragement to Gerald.

24 September

TGRD   The automatic suspension of Steve Bainbridge from International selection to the English team is unfairly harsh. To be sent off the field is in itself embarrassing. To be stopped instantly from playing any more rugby until the case is heard and sentence passed is ignominious and frustrating. This is what the ordinary player receives. In England there is an automatic thirty-day suspension and for the International player the further humiliation of not being considered for the National team for the remainder of the season. So Bainbridge has to sit it out for the whole season. It is a case of heaping up retribution, like Greek tragedy, until it exceeds the original crime. And sentence is passed without the case being heard. The referee is the sole judge of fact according to the laws and so it should be on the field of play. But, and it is a big 'but', he is not so right that an objection cannot be raised and the player's case put forward. And it must be borne in mind that standards of interpretation can and do vary from district to district, from referee to referee, and what is one man's meat is another man's poison. Whatever they may say at the RFU on this matter, the Welsh disciplinary procedure is more reasonable. Each case of sending off is considered individually and the punishment can range from a three-week suspension to a life ban. Any Welsh squad player sent off has his name removed from the squad and not put forward for selection until he has served his sentence.

TGRD   Down to Swansea to see the Whites play the Dublin club, Lansdowne. Not the most entertaining game – it will take another month to get into full swing. But it astonishes me to see the precocious style of scrum-half Robert Jones, still only nineteen, not rewarded more. He confirms what was seen of him last year. Here is a player in the making who should surely be included in this season's Welsh squad, a youngster who could well take over the mantle of Holmes when he decides to call it a day. Let him rub shoulders with the elite now and give him encouragement before it is too late. But, alas, the one Welsh selector at St. Helen's to whom I suggested this says he has no time for him at this stage. Is this another of those doors they are so fond of shutting?

3

October

Our backs are fast as motor-cyclists, all our forwards weigh
    twenty stone.
Each of them can score unaided, running strongly on his own.
Gavin Ewart

5 October

TGRD The way Pontypool is playing the journey to
Pontypool Park is likely to be repeated quite a few times
this season. After the first month they are the team
making all the running and after ten matches are the only
unbeaten club left in Wales. Already they have brushed
aside Newport and Bridgend with contemptuous ease, if
such a phrase is appropriate for a team so utterly without
vanity, and on Wednesday last they overcame Swansea
at St. Helen's. There is a merciless inevitability about
Pontypool's play. They are supremely efficient and dedi-
cated in getting and keeping their hands on the ball.
When they kick, they kick well.

Largely because of the influence of Eddie Butler, they
are a disciplined team these days which, if anything,
makes them even more awesome as they dissect the
opposition's more vulnerable parts. And it occurs to me
it does not really matter, apart from Bishop at scrum-half,
who exactly makes up the numbers in the team. Against
Bridgend they had the inexperienced Moreton and a
mere slip of a lad, Carter, last year's Secondary School's
captain, at lock. Other clubs might have offered excuses
for a depleted side. Not Pontypool. They simply carried
on as before.

It is a style which invariably prompts a contemptuous

groan and can infuriate and arouse admiration in equal measures. After all, they are good at what they do. They achieve what they set out to achieve, week in, week out. Of how many clubs, and of how many coaches, can that be said? Pontypool make no extravagant claims for their rugby. It is other clubs who do that.

Coaches often profess in high moral tone that their own clubs embrace the open handling game. Yet, to observe those teams in action is often to give the lie to their claims.

It is high time another coach came along who can demonstrate his fine philosophy on the field of play as successfully as Ray Prosser has so assiduously found expression for his over the last fifteen years.

6 October

JM What seems a commonplace match like Neath against Llanelli today evokes so much. I saw Lewis Jones, a player of genius, in his first match for Neath when he was only seventeen. As he describes it in his autobiography *King of Rugger* (Stanley Paul, 1958): "fortune was doubly kind to me on that cold January afternoon at the Gnoll ground, for not only was I able to contribute twelve of the twenty-four points that were the margin of Neath's victory, but the Welsh selectors were there." Lewis Jones' book is one of the best ever written by a rugby player and is too much neglected by bibliophiles of the game. His analysis of the role of the full-back as an attacking force is well ahead of his time; his delight in scoring more while tackling less is central to the best tradition. Those of us who saw him were lucky.

Those of us who went to grammar schools in South Wales may see both Neath and Llanelli slightly differently from the experience of those who support the town sides who did not. Both grammar schools were so well-organised. I used to captain a Swansea Grammar School side playing Neath. We seemed like amateurs. At which it crosses my mind that I always seemed to be captain. That's how I was in the team. I wasn't a good player, but I was always the captain. It was the same in the RAF. In life I'm told I tend to be a rather ebullient, some would say over-theatrical, kind of character. As a player I was the most boring back ever seen on the field. As an outside-half, people used to swear at me. I wouldn't give anybody the ball because I was sure we were going to lose it. I think I was only tolerated because I was the goal kicker. One RAF team I was in did have two Internationals in the three-quarter line to whom I would give the ball. Was it that I didn't trust my schoolmates? Or is there something in the nature of the game which demands that style contradicts character? I certainly was a boring player. A captain doesn't have to be.

12 October

TGRD   When all is said and done, and in Wales at least as far as rugby is concerned, it cannot all be said, nor is it ever likely to be completely done, the laws of the game still need some revision. They are an inexhaustible source of debate. No wonder the clubs and pubs are full and the breweries have made their fortunes.

One of the strongest arguments against rugby becoming a professional sport – should such an unlikely proposal as was made by David Lord last year ever be revised – is that the laws of the game remain far too inequitable and too difficult to maintain the degree of uniformity that such status would demand. The best professional sports are those in which a clearer sense of purpose and intent leaves little room for doubt. Rugby remains a game full of grey areas. No one can be certain what dark deeds are committed in a scrum. And for every infringement that the referee sees at the line-out and penalises, the spectators see a dozen more. Could professional careers be allowed to hang on such threads of doubt? What would fifteen McEnroes do in these circumstances?

Two recent games are indicative of the flaws. In a match between Pontypool and Swansea ten days ago forty-three penalties were awarded. Last Wednesday when Bridgend met Cardiff there were thirty-seven. And yet at a match at the end of last season between Bridgend and Llanelli, with the same laws applying, Clive Norling, who in all honesty is not averse to bringing his authority to bear on any game, awarded only six. Such discrepancy reflects not so much on the referee or the players but rather on the laws themselves, where technical infringements are seen to be on a par with foul play. There are laws which contrive to frustrate player and spectator alike. That a knock-on can incur a penalty if it is deemed to be deliberate is nonsensical. And shoulder-high tackles are penalised regardless of whether they are dangerous or not. Talking to referees Winston Jones and Derek Bevan about the matter of the knock-on, they both almost in unison said that coaches these days come up to complain to them if they do not award penalties in these circumstances. I still think it is a foolish law and my answer to the coaches would be to do their job properly and to teach their players to time their passes more accurately, so there is less risk of interception.

The tackle law remains the most unsatisfactory part of the game. The tackler and the tackled are often subject to an unfair interpretation. In the smother tackle, the tackler can be penalised for inadvertently falling over on the wrong side as a result of his momentum. And the tackled man can be punished for not releasing the ball when he may be hindered from doing so by the very nature of that kind of tackle. It goes against the spirit of the game, too, if the tackled man, brought down to one knee, say, is not allowed to pass the ball so as to continue the attack, but is forced to release it by placing the ball on the ground.

Why should 'release' be interpreted in so limited a fashion? Why can't a player 'release' by handing on to another supporting player?

Although the laws, or rather the notes to the laws, suggest that, if the referee is in doubt, a scrummage should be awarded, invariably a penalty is given. Such a law continues to frustrate rather than advance the claim of rugby to be a handling game. Clive Norling maintains that there is little divergence in interpretation of the laws, but that there is a substantial difference in their application.

17 October

TGRD   Too many games, the cry goes up. True, there's too much high-level competition in sport. Rugby is becoming as bad as cricket. As one set of tourists departs another is on the way. It's high time the whole thing was rationalised. But the administrators turn a blind eye to the extra pressures and fix their gaze on the cash flow.

Now the 7th Wallabies have arrived and we look forward to their eighteen matches. The nonstop tour circus makes it tempting to draw up unofficial merit tables. Where will the Australians stand if they have a successful tour? In the Bledisloe Cup they have already played the All Blacks (who had earlier beaten France) and put up a good performance, only being narrowly beaten in a three-match series. England lost in South Africa last summer, and will travel to New Zealand in the summer of 1985, after which the All Blacks will themselves go to South Africa, as also will the Lions in 1986.

The logical end of all this frenetic touring must surely be a World Cup. With so many countries now playing rugby football, a structure which incorporates them all is needed in a rapidly changing rugby world where the concept of a British Lions team will fast become an anachronism.

TGRD   Once more Terry Holmes' rugby career has been cruelly interrupted. Last night mid-way through the second half of the match between Cardiff and Pontypool, and in front of 17,000, the largest crowd ever to assemble at the Cardiff club ground – they were literally hanging from the rafters and twice those standing on the rickety club offices were asked to come down off the roof – he walked disconsolately off the Arms Park with a dislocated shoulder, a recurrence of an injury which first troubled him on the Lions tour to South Africa in 1980 and from which, after surgery, he took a long time to recover.

The injury occurred when he tackled Chris Huish, the Pontypool flanker. "Such was the speed and commitment of both players into the tackle," Eddie Butler, the Pontypool captain said, "that something had to give. Sadly, it was a serious injury to Terry." At the hospital he needed a general anaesthetic. It looks as if he will be away for at least two months.

Considering the number of games that Terry Holmes plays, it is astonishing how he has remained relatively free of those niggling minor ailments which afflict a player during the season. Yet three times now he has suffered more serious setbacks. Apart from his previous dislocation, there was the damaged knee in the first International against New Zealand in 1983 which took ten months to recover. He returned to take part in only the final International against England last season. His flaw, if it can be so called, is that he has not yet been able to measure his game. There had been signs that with his new responsibility as captain, he was beginning to learn the value of economy. But his uninhibited enthusiasm for rugby is such that he always feels the need to play in top gear, at a pace which has taken its toll on his hefty and athletic frame. The irony is that he might have been better off had he suffered the occasional twinge or strained muscle that others bear. Then he would have been forced to restrict the number of games he plays.

Now the Welsh selectors face a repeat of last year's dilemma, as to who should replace him. On the statistical evidence of tries and points scored and the huge contribution he makes to Pontypool, David Bishop is in line to inherit, however briefly, the No. 9 jersey. If that comes to pass, last year's Welsh strategy of running wide would need to be abandoned and any discussion of the talent at stand-off, or the merits of the centre and wings, will be purely academic, such is his fondness for doing things his way. And what of Mark Douglas and Ray Giles? I still think it is time to look to the long-term future by introducing young Robert Jones of Swansea into the squad. We need to groom someone now, not necessarily for this year, but for next year and the year after.

21 October

TGRD   The Welsh squad is announced in preparation for the Australian match. In time-honoured fashion, and to cover themselves for their sins of omission, the selectors reserve the right to bring others into the squad as they see fit. No Gareth Davies. The old prejudice still lives and, I have no doubt, he can consider his International days are over whilst the present coaches are in place. They are not flexible enough and have a tendency to shut the door too early. I'm not sure that they can detect talent either. Apart from the exclusion of Gareth Davies, why no Glen Webbe of Bridgend on the wing? If they do not give him any recognition soon, it will be too late. A hint of reward is invaluable to the rising star. And the fact that Swansea's Robert Jones must still wait for the call is made the more ridiculous by there being no less than four scrum-halves in the squad – Terry Holmes, David

45

Bishop, Mark Douglas and Ray Giles. What is the point of including four scrum-halves? Some indecision or muddled thinking here.

23 October

JM How strong the custom is in Wales, which is nice, for women to buy rugby books for men. I was bought Alun Richards' study of Carwyn James today in Swansea by a friend: it was my fifty-fifth birthday; Carwyn whom I had known since the mid-forties was coeval. I had been booked to stay in the hotel in Amsterdam in which he died two weeks after that sad end. I changed hotels. Two weeks before he died we had exchanged drinks and cigarettes in the BBC Club in Cardiff. He and I were the only two people we knew who still smoked untipped Senior Service, a legacy, we thought, of our service days, his Navy, in my case, RAF. We always would agree that there was no point in smoking unless the fags had quality: they had to be a real smoke. I went into a village in the Wye Valley lately and asked the tobacconist for Senior Service. He told me: "I used to sell a lot of them, but not any more, because my customers have all died." Carwyn died before I could tell him that tale.

It was playing against Carwyn in a schools' match in the 'forties that made me realise that there was a class I could not aspire to. In the 'fifties, when I was writing about rugby for *The Observer* I would report as often as seemed unbiased about his revelatory performances at outside-half for Llanelli and the manner in which he was creating an exuberant and delightful style of play. People who admire his intellectual gifts and his subsequent achievements forget how dazzling a player he was for so long. Like his inheritor, Barry John, he was never tackled; neither would he demean himself by tackling. That Llanelli team of the 'fifties understood rugby. Their Carwyn was a prince: no one must touch him.

During his playing career Carwyn would call around and drink a cup of tea with us in Swansea. He was not then the gin-and-tonic man he later became celebrated as. We would talk more about poetry and Welsh nationalism than rugby. In the late 'seventies he agreed to be my guest, or oppo, as we put it, when I had a BBC Radio arts programme and was keen to launch a new Welsh magazine *Arcade* with some publicity. An audience expecting some forceful analysis of the game were briefly puzzled at my references to an Arcadian culture, and Carwyn's quite brilliant response with quotations from Welsh poetry, ancient and modern.

The last time I saw him, a few weeks before he died, he asked me if I had remembered a chat we'd had in the 'fifties about what we wanted to do with our lives. I said I did. I had said that I'd like to write a few books that might make people laugh and see the world as we saw it. And he had said he would like people to play the sort of rugby that would give pleasure and see the game as he saw it. As he wrapped his sad, eczema-troubled hands one in the other, and looked so unhappy, I said he'd made it.

23 October

TGRD   And so, who is there now? It was that perceptive Englishman, Bill Redwood, former Bristol scrum-half, who observed that despite the many ills besetting the British game, everything would be all right in the end as long as Carwyn James was around. (Is it significant it took an Englishman to honour Wales's prophet?)

Three long years have now passed with what would appear to be three long barren winters. What optimism is there these days? Who is there to inspire? And to whom can we turn? "We need to encourage the cult of the coach," he once said to a congress of coaches who, smiling, took him at his word. Sadly, their vision was not Carwyn's vision. Or if it was, they have left a miserable trail of failure.

In Oxford in the 'thirties they divided university society, arbitrarily, into aesthetes and hearties. There were a very few who refused to accept the cultural fracture and walked in both worlds. In Wales Carwyn was one such all his life. And at the end of it all those memorial services were a microcosm of the many-faceted life he had led. It was in his empathy with a multitude of friends from all walks of life that lay the secret of his success as a coach. He appreciated the aesthetes as much as the hearties, and they did him. Though the poetry in him outweighed the prose, he found the common ground of understanding. He was sensitive to all our moods.

Who of today's coaches responds to the man who has his point to make? And who is alert to the man with independent flair? Who feels equally at home with 'Eskimo Nell' and 'Myfanwy' in the same team? Can the dreamer and the joker, the pen-pusher and the boiler-maker make it too? You need to be faithful to them all in your fashion. And they to you. He was admirably and amiably cool, they said. He had the good sense. But it was his generous sensibility that set him apart and will forever set him a league and more away from the drifting bottom of good sense of the rest.

Being of the old, respectable school he saw rugby as a thinking man's game and reared on the radical tradition of the Welshman's hearth he was brought up not to believe everything he read in books. It was a potent mix, which saw the classical style tied to the romantic; the orthodox mixing with mischief and cunning.

In his long impenetrable silences Carwyn knew rugby's mysteries and subtleties. And in his talk he admitted the simplicities. He valued cunning and light-hearted mischief, and in a cloud of cigarette smoke in an Auckland stand he knew the fear the prospect of failure

48

brings. To survive was to live by your wits, and to win was due to a God-given talent to amuse – or could simply be put down to accident. It might even be stimulated by the weather taking a sudden change for the worse or, perhaps by half time, for the better – a good fine day for experts on their toes; a bad one for the simple morality of the bone-crusher. It is, after all, a flawed game.

Above all he knew those players in a team who could stand alone and those who could not, those who needed a word of encouragement and those who didn't.

If he knew us, did we know him?

He knew the joy, as we knew his joy, but after reading Alun Richards' perceptive memoir, one is left with an underlying sense of a life disappointed, even of despair. A solitary mister.

24 October

TGRD   Today Cardiff beat the Wallabies. But it will be a rash man who writes the tourists off for this so early in their progress. Cardiff are a very strong side with nine Internationals who would fancy their chances against any of the teams in the Five Nations Championship except France. And what yet can we really know about the various National sides for this season?

Bearing in mind what happened last year and his continued exclusion from the present squad, Gareth Davies is likely to prove an embarrassment to the Welsh selectors this season. Why close the door so emphatically on him? They seem to have rejected him altogether, which might not be very clever in the long run. He had a marvellous game against the Australians today and was the main architect of Cardiff's victory. After his performance against the tourists there should be no doubt that he is the best outside-half playing in Wales and perhaps even the British Isles. But for those who matter, the

49

selectors, he is, ridiculously, no more than fifth in line of succession. Ahead of him are Malcolm Dacey, Geraint John, Jonathan Davies, and Paul Turner. For other countries looking in it must be a source of envy that there is such a wealth of choice available to us, but the way we squander our wealth must be a great comfort to them. Gareth Davies's exclusion from the Welsh squad almost amounts to a miscarriage of justice.

25 October

TGRD   I rang Gareth to write a piece for *The Times*.

"I must admit," he said, "that I was on the verge of quitting the game a few weeks ago. I wasn't playing all that well at the very start of the season and since I was being ignored at National level, there was no incentive to improve my game. I am still ambitious to get back into the Welsh team. Playing at this level for Cardiff, it is natural to want to reach for higher honours but the way things were going there seemed no hope of that ever happening."

It was his club mate, Alan Phillips, another player inexplicably discarded from Welsh considerations, who convinced him that he ought to stay on.

"You're a long time in retirement and you're a long time dead, when you have no choice in the matter, is the way Alan put it to me," said Gareth who took his mate's word and decided to carry on playing. "I have had a word with the selectors and one of them maintains that I don't tackle. He also picked out one incident in a game when I should have fallen on the ball, got up, and set up a maul or something. When they hold things like that against me I must admit that I am baffled. I don't entirely agree with the idea that I don't tackle. I believe that the stand-off is of more value to the team if he can stay on his feet than if he's caught in the middle of a ruck or maul.'

Which, I must admit, is the way that Barry John used to put it. "Why else have wing forwards?" was the way he answered his critics.

4

November

One is always more vexed at losing a game of any sort by a single hole or ace, than if one has never had a chance of winning it.

William Hazlitt

10 November

TGRD   I've never been convinced of the value of Wales B games. Some of my more well-heeled friends however entertain no such misgivings as they take the trip, every other year, to France to enjoy as happily bloated epicureans, all the good things that places like Bourg-en-Bresse have to offer. I don't get the impression they are as enthusiastic as all that about the home match in, say, Aberavon or Newport. The game this year played at Rodney Parade is the sixteenth in the series which began in the 1969/70 season. To date 162 players have played in the series which only allows uncapped players and a total of sixty-eight have gone on to play in the Welsh senior team. The size of that figure surprises me, bearing in mind that it covers the 1970s when the side was considered to be a settled one. Of the Welsh team which finished the season at Twickenham in March 1984, twelve had progressed via this Wales B route which must, therefore, be considered as a useful stepping stone. Holmes, Hadley and Bowen were the three who had not.

So far, France have won nine of the encounters to Wales' six. In the first nine games victory went to the home side. France broke the sequence in the tenth when they won 31-18 at Aberavon in 1978/79, a success which was repeated in 1982/83 at Pontypool. Wales' only away win came last year in Bourg-en-Bresse under the leadership of Mike Watkins who, largely because of that exploit, got his first full cap and the captaincy of the senior team later last year. France have accumulated 275 points altogether, Wales 235, France having scored thirty-nine tries to Wales' twenty-three, although for what it is worth the penalty count goes in Wales' favour by thirty-six to twenty-two. It was of some concern that Wales had managed only one try in six matches from 1977 until last year when, with relief, they scored four.

Of more interest to the selectors than these bald statistics is the way the players conduct themselves and perform one step away from the International arena proper. Jonathan Davies (outside-half) from Neath, Gareth Roberts (flanker) from Cardiff, and David Bishop (scrum-half) from Pontypool are the players who are taking tentative steps today, in the hope of going on to higher things.

12 November

TGRD   Yes, all three did well and no doubt they will make some contribution this year, if only to the debate . . .

But, of more interest than this match, which Wales won in rather lucky circumstances by 29-20, was the second victory for the Australians by 16-9 at Lansdowne Road, having beaten England 19-3 last week. Half way through their Test schedule and they are two up in the series which is apparently the first time this has happened in thirty-seven years. This confirms my unwillingness to write them off after the Cardiff game. All the same, I did not really expect this clear cut authority and dominance from Australia. I still fancy Wales' chances with the right selection at half-back and in the back row, however. Our scrum should be superior too.

TGRD   Nostalgia is built into the woodwork of rugby clubs. Deep in his cups a fearsome prop of yesteryear will reminisce about how his old friends played, reliving the games in a soft focus quite alien to his hard, core-of-steel reputation. And you might as well believe him because the past he remembers so rosily is just as likely to be in store for you.

The physical shrine for all this nostalgia is the club's trophy cabinet, and there's nothing quite like the collection they have down at Carmarthen Athletic Club, who have just drawn Pontypool in the first round of the Schweppes Cup.

Their President, Gwynne Morgan, is a chemist who lives with his elder brother in the oldest inhabited building in Carmarthen. Gwynne is the kind of person who has the habit of turning up in the unlikeliest of places and often within shoulder-rubbing distance of the famous. The long-standing joke in Carmarthen is that if he appeared in St. Peter's Square in Rome people would wonder who it was in the white robes standing next to Gwynne Morgan. His passion is collecting sporting memorabilia for the club of which he has now been President for twenty-three years. It has put him in touch with all the great names of sport, and not only rugby. There are now 120 jerseys, but it's the wall full of boots of the famous that makes Carmarthen Athletic's trophy haul unique.

The boot-collecting venture all began, Gwynne tells you solemnly, because of the foot and mouth disease scare of 1967. He and the then club Chairman, Eric Clarke, had travelled to Cardiff to present Brian Lochore's All Blacks with a miniature coracle as a memento of their visit. And they especially wanted to honour that great man, Colin Meads, who had been sent off at Murrayfield the previous Saturday. Meads was so overcome that anyone should want to comfort him in such a way, especially in Wales, that he ran upstairs to fetch his boots and presented them to the club. Mac Herewini did the same. "Because of the foot and mouth, you see, they could not take them back to New Zealand anyway," Gwynne says with a glint in his eye. His boot fetish then really took off. The prime position in the club's centre cabinet is occupied by the pair that gives Gwynne the most satisfaction – the white boots which once belonged to Muhammad Ali. They were procured for him by Gerald Williams, the BBC tennis commentator who hails from nearby Llanstephan. Here hang Cooper's and Conteh's boots; Beckenbauer and Pele represent one footballing generation, Finney and John Charles another; Cowdrey and Sobers, Botham and Richards are there. So are Thompson, Ovett and Coe, Nastasie, Borg and Billie Jean King; and of course anybody who was anybody in rugby over the last twenty years has his boots here, with autograph and good wishes attached.

Which was the most difficult pair to obtain?

"I couldn't for the life of me get hold of Sir Stanley Matthews. Whenever I rang, I spoke to his wife who had learnt as every wife does, she said, to expect him when she saw him. That was the time he had commitments in South Africa, Canada and Malta. It was difficult."

But Gwynne has a way of making an offer that no one has yet refused.

"Would you like a salmon, Lady Matthews, fresh from the Towy?" he asked.

"Oh, yes please. We have some Scots friends coming down," came the reply. Which is all the opening he wanted. The fish was immediately despatched by British Rail. The boots duly arrived a week later.

The catch that gives him the most pleasure? Sir Gordon Richards is his unhesitating nomination. Horse racing, too, has been a passion with Gwynne Morgan. There was a time when he owned fifteen thoroughbreds and he is one of an elite to have had a winner, Olympus, at Cheltenham trained by the owner.

"Again there was a difficulty," he said. "Sir Gordon had given all his gear away. Don't bother, I was told." But that was the sort of challenge Gwynne can't resist. Away went another British Rail parcel with, by now, the familiar contents. The recipient scoured the attic and found a pair of boots. The letter which accompanied the gift is there in the cabinet, and says they were the pair Sir Gordon wore for his Derby winner, Pinza.

Nothing is ordinary in Gwynne's world. When I saw him today he was preparing to go on the maiden voyage of the *Royal Princess.* And I wonder which sporting megastar he would manage to relieve of his footwear on the cruise.

[As it turned out he met up with Mike and his wife, landlord of one of my locals, the Nag's Head, in Usk. They had a rough passage, I understood, and spent a sleepless night in each other's company at the bar. In the course of which Gwynne discovered that Mike had a pair of Jack Peterson's boxing gloves. Not just any old pair but the ones with which he had put away Walter Neusel. Needless to say by the end of that storm, off the coast of Florida, the gloves had been promised to the Athletic Club. They now hang there.]

Pontypool won comfortably and afterwards Jeff Squire handed over his boots as another contribution to the very special Boot Hill of Wales' Far West overlooking the Towy and the M4.

16 November

TGRD The Welsh team to play the Wallabies is announced. This will give an indication of the way things are likely to go for the rest of the season. After two years in office nothing is so predictable as the unpredictability of the present selectors. They also give the impression of stubbornness. 'Intransigent' is Clem Thomas' word for them.

Moriarty is still serving his period of suspension after being sent off against Llanelli. So with their infinite capacity to surprise and cause occasional anxiety, they have chosen Alun Davies of Llanelli to play at this level after only three appearances this season because of pneumonia. The need to counteract Australia's line-out has determined that he, being the taller man, should get the place ahead of Gareth Roberts who performed so well for Wales B last Saturday. In the absence of Holmes, Bishop gets the scrum-half position.

Gareth Davies remains in the wilderness which, after his superlative performance for Cardiff against Australia, will give comfort to Alan Jones, the Australian coach. This will put considerable pressure on Malcolm Dacey who has yet to find his best form, and only last week returned to the game after injury.

I am surprised, too, at the inclusion of Mark Wyatt, not for lack of ability as such, but because there is very little that separates him from Howell Davies of Bridgend. The latter is the man in possession and he did score thirty-nine points in the Championship last season. It is difficult to see the reasoning behind this decision. Davies is probably the better attacker, though Wyatt is better under the high ball. It is the inconsistency in selection here that bothers me.

24 November

TGRD   Wales 9, Australia 28.

This, as the score amply demonstrates, was an over-whelming win for the tourists. And, more worryingly for Wales, they were worth every point of it. There was no special rub of the green that went Australia's way, no hard-luck story for the Welsh to tell. There were no chances missed which might have swung the game the other way; no refereeing indecision. It was quite emphatic.

In the end there was no Welsh player who came near to filling the socks of his Australian counterpart; each was made to look a grade lower than his opposite number. And it is a grade that now separates at least three of the Home Countries from those in the southern hemisphere. A gap has reappeared of the kind which existed in the early 'sixties. It is a critical time for Wales' game.

The Australian display indicates that this team can be compared not only to their own country's best standards of the past, but to the more exacting ones of the recent All Blacks. Australian teams have always included individual world-class players but here for the first time is a team which has matured into a unit, one which does not deny the individual's flair, and is aware of all the tactical implications of what they do. They are athletic, sharp, quick-witted and enterprising. Like the All Black teams who came to Wales in the centenary year, they make Wales look ponderous and old-fashioned. Not only did the Australians score more points, they inflicted the most telling and embarrassing blow which no other side has done in recent memory by scoring a pushover try. The scrum, after all, was meant to be the dominating preserve of the Welsh.

In the five years which separate the All Blacks tour from the Wallabies no discernible advance has been made in Wales. The game is in desperate need of a new stimulation.

These Wallabies on one level have highlighted that we cannot match them for fitness and athleticism. This, set alongside a moribund tactical sense, emphasises Wales' present predicament. Coaches appear to be set in their ways, clubs are weighed down with too many fixtures. Too much coaching of an inferior standard, too many games, too many squads. Too much of everything. Quality has been sacrificed for quantity. New ideas tend to be superimposed on what already exists. For example, those who advised the WRU on fitness programmes a few seasons ago added their ideas on to what is already happening in the clubs, and the programme was not tailored to the specific needs and demands of rugby as it is currently organised.

Wales will no doubt do well in this year's Championship but no one should be under any illusion as to what that means. The first division will be found elsewhere. But let's seek promotion and come top of that division.

30 November

TGRD   The hoary old consolation that the Welsh team never finds its form until after Christmas should not be wheeled out, as it predictably is in some quarters, to answer for the Australian defeat last week. If that were the case, Welsh chances against touring sides would be bleak indeed. There ought to be greater pride in admitting defeat. We then know our standard. What are squad training sessions for if not to prepare the player, in all aspects, for International competition whenever it occurs?

In terms of match fitness, most clubs in Wales will have played around twenty-five matches by Christmas, which will be more, for example, than many a New Zealand club will play in a full season. A club there will play at best twenty divisional matches, with a provincial championship providing an additional seven for the better players. These are obligatory, others can be arranged on a 'friendly' basis. While it would not be practicable to imitate another country's system wholesale, there is a tendency in Wales in the present set-up to mistake quantity for quality. Is the game so institutionalised in Wales that it is not possible to introduce any radical changes?

5

December

8 December

TGRD   Scotland went down to the rollercoaster Australian team and thus they complete the Grand Slam. Alan
Jones is always ready with the nicely turned phrase.
After the Welsh game, when they had efficiently overcome what may have appeared beforehand as the most
formidable of the obstacles, he was asked about his
thoughts for the Grand Slam with the easier prospect of
beating Scotland to come. He replied, "You know, one
day you can be the rooster and the next the feather
duster. We won't crow for a little while yet."

And what did he have to say after the final victory? "A
lot of hard work has gone into the tour. There's been a lot
of sweat in the training sessions. And it's all come right.
Like a pair of Gucci shoes, you still have them and can
admire the quality long after you've forgotten the price
you paid for them." The Australian players will remember the glory long after they've forgotten the sweat and
the pain.

12 December

JM   Setting off to watch Pontypool play Australia I had
to abandon the trip because of fog. I rang the ground and
was told there was heavy mist there and so thought that
on television the match would probably be visible: the

camera has a greater capacity than the human eye to cut through fog. Why this should be I do not know. The match was dull, as games at Pontypool often are, but it was clear that the Australian forwards were quite capable of holding the powerful Welsh club team. When their forwards are held, then Pontypool seem short of ideas, while the Australians played the home International scrum-half, Bishop, out of the match. All season the inclination has been to consider the visitors a fine back division: the pack was truly a source of strength today.

While dimly discerning the play through the fog, a friend offered a tale about a Welsh rugby forward, a famous donkey of the team. One such, a wealthy entrepreneur nowadays, had been on holiday in Rhodes. At Lindos he had approached the man in charge of hiring donkeys to climb the steps to the acropolis. Here was this huge Welshman, here the small donkey. The hirer demurred, believing the donkey would collapse in carrying the heavyweight. The Welshman explained that the Greek did not understand and so demonstrated. He lifted the donkey, put the animal on his back and carried it up the steps.

14 December

TGRD   I doubt whether rugby held many charms for Neville Cardus. But a good deal of what he perceived to be the essence of his game's character and the variety of its appeal can often be seen in rugby. "Go among the shilling crowd one fine day," he once wrote of the Oval, "and what do you hear? Little technical jargon, little talk of off-breaks and the position of the left funny bone in the left cut." No, the overall effect was what mattered to him; the completeness of the beautiful stroke.

And I do not suppose that the position of the funny bone, the shoulder or the exact spacing of the feet in the ruck matters much to the man on the tanner bank at Stradey, St. Helen's or in Eugene Cross Park. Although there is the tackle he can savour and the sinister magic of the side-step, it is the general impression of these that appeals. It is the completeness, the rounded perfection of it all.

The art of any game is to conceal the artifice; not to give the game away by showing your intentions. The player's art, like the actor's art, should not reveal the energy and the thought, the sweat and the spit, that have gone into the rehearsal. Nor should the anxiety surface from beneath the skin.

The Australians made their game look easy and natural. The observer was not aware of the detail, only of the overall colourful impression.

The trouble with our domestic game is that too many of our players look as if they have been reading too many books and have brought their theories with them on to the field. As each forward bends his head and dips his shoulder, as each three-quarter labours along his path and the crash move follows, they do so painfully in the shadow of the textbook. Or perhaps in the shadow of the coach who has read the textbook. Cardus might recognise the 'funny-bone syndrome'.

These thoughts are made more acute after seeing this year's entertaining Varsity match on Tuesday last which Cambridge won in some style. For the British game, the most inspiring moment of the week came in that match as the students, particularly Cambridge, for once ignored the textbook. It was not Bailey's run and swivel, marvellous though they were, that one remembers most, nor Hastings' sprint or Simms actually scoring the first try, but that very lonely moment for Andrew when he bravely changed his mind, ignored the obvious and, triumphantly, took the calculated risk on his own 22-metre line. A poignant moment, for there was a lot of forgotten British rugby in that.

TGRD   Barbarians v. Australia – a game which was marred by some poor refereeing. M. Hourquet was far too lax. He allowed himself too loose an interpretation of the laws and this took away a good deal from the game as a contest and, in the end, as a spectacle too. There were tries scored which involved not one obvious infringement, but two or three. This was particularly unfortunate as the Barbarians carried the burden of British rugby on their shoulders after the Grand Slam of victories inflicted on the Home Countries by the Australians. And they started off so well and looked set to make a match of it, where no one had expected anything of the kind from a scratch side.

The first invitation I received to play for the Baa-baas was quite stark. Addressed 'Dear Davies', as if summoning me to appear in front of someone who was bound to make me feel less than honourable, it asked me to bring along my boots and club stockings. I checked the invitation card, with its unmistakably colourful motif which accompanied the letter, to see whether it included my initials. There are a lot of us Davieses in Wales. Did they have the right bloke in mind? They did. I don't think I waited, as was my arrogant custom in later years, until a call came for me to confirm my availability. I answered, as they say, forthwith. Being addressed in that way does have a salutary effect and prompts an immediate reply. It was an honour and a pleasure, for goodness' sake, to play for the Barbarians. Any club which can incorporate Geoff Wheel and 'Charlie' Faulkner dressed as char ladies singing 'There's a hole in my bucket, dear Liza, dear Liza' and Charlie Kent playing a Chopin sonata on the same after-dinner billing must have something going for it which is unique.

Its maverick qualities, with no headquarters, no club house, no pitch, no finances and no interminable committee meetings may be the envy of all. Tradition and precedence are its guiding principles and the joy of attacking rugby is the tie that binds. Like a rogue elephant, it is part of the species, but because of its eccentricities, remains splendidly independent. Self-indulgent one moment, generous the next. Exclusive, yet they acknowledge no boundaries.

There are some who would claim that the adventurous Barbarian approach is becoming an anachronism in the new realism that pervades much of our rugby today and the harsh realities of intensified competition. And yet the time invariably comes when the Barbarians prick the consciences of us all. Players, relieved of their club or National responsibilities, happily forget the stereotyped response and react more in accordance with what their instincts tell them. Their flamboyance and panache make us wonder about the rhymes and rhythms of a game which becomes jaded with too much analysis. At their best they provide a vision of what is possible. They can surprise, move us and make our spines tingle.

This evening I am invited to the official dinner at the Royal Hotel in Cardiff. In the gents I happen to meet Jeff Whitefoot, the Cardiff prop who was on the replacement bench this afternoon. He said he had not enjoyed a game so much in a long time. Considering that he had not played, I took the irony. But he was quite serious. He had not been so relaxed, he had not known the enjoyment of being part of a team, at this level before. There had been no training as such. They had got together, played some touch rugby, gone through a few moves, jogged around a bit and then retired for a relaxing drink in Jackson's in Westgate Street. The Barbarians, a scratch team, had played with more enterprise and style than any of the National teams who had spent weeks in preparation. Something is fundamentally wrong with the game and the way it is presently coached if players are so ready to go against the current tenets of coaching. There seems to be a gap between what the players need, and what the coaches think they ought to have.

This seemed to be confirmed when I got back to the table. A discussion was in full flow, the general drift of which was that the Australians have left British rugby nursing an inferiority complex. "What if our approach to coaching is wrong?" asked Northampton's Don White. He looked comfortably genial in a way he could not possibly have looked to his opponents at the bottom of a ruck those many years ago. He'd had to confront that question over three decades ago when, as a great captain of the formidable Northampton club of those days, his team, based on a powerful pack, came up against Bleddyn Williams' free-running Cardiff. After the defeat White admitted that he had to reconsider his ideas and that there might be another way to play.

The question no longer applies, as it did then, simply on a local level. It has far wider implications. Since those times when White and Williams could quite happily have applied their ideas independently of each other and with equal validity, the game, in fact, has changed very little. The laws have been tinkered with, so that as one new law seems to quicken up the game, something else of the players' or the coaches' contrivance will be found to slow it down. Swings and roundabouts apply to rugby as in much else. What *has* had a significant effect on the game in this country is, of course, the development of coaching at all levels. This has generally been for the good. The difficulty now is that it has become so conventional and institutionalised. Whatever happens in Hawick will more than likely be repeated in Haverfordwest, from Fylde to Falmouth, from Selkirk to Skerries.

This, it could be argued, might help forge a common bond of understanding, which might be advantageous to the likes of the Barbarians. But in the case of the Lions it has been less than impressive on the last three tours and all sorts of excuses were found for those failures.

"What if we are wrong?" asks Don White. It is those Home Unions and their staff coaches who address themselves to answering Don White's question who are likely to reap the rewards.

21 December

TGRD   Mike Watkins, the Welsh captain, has made the dramatic announcement via his solicitor that he no longer wants to play for Wales. This is within hours of being named in the Welsh squad preparing for the Five Nations Championship and less than a year after winning his first cap. At thirty-two years of age he had won four caps, the first against Ireland last year when he was also made captain. He will still captain the Newport side. He is a great character, a good solid man to have around on the field – one of those to have in the trenches, as it were.

He played for Cardiff at a time when I was captain, and he had to compete for his place in the team with another expert hooker, Alan Phillips. I have never been warm to the idea of keeping players on rota. It is my belief that it is better to make a decision one way or the other. It doesn't do the players any good to know that they will play alternate matches. Both Cardiff hookers were very good at their tasks, albeit different ones. Mike, or Spikey, was efficient as a mauler, always wanting to be in the thick of things to rip the ball away. He was an expert, especially in those days when the maul played a prominent, if to a degree negative, role in the Welsh game, and jersey rolled up to the elbows, he thrived on it. Alan thrived on a looser type of game, a runner, a supporter, but certainly not one who thereby ignored the essentials of a rugby forward's chores. They differed not in degree but in kind.

It happened that I came down in favour of Alan Phillips. And I then had the task of telling Spikey of the decision. I did so at the Pontypool club after one of our matches there. Being aware of his special talent, I suggested that his rugby career might be better served if he went to play in the first team at another club. Not that I wanted to encourage him to do so, but I tried to explain that, if he did so, then I would understand. Typical of the man, he stayed to compete for the place at Cardiff, serving the club for five or six more years altogether.

There is the other side of his contribution. For all the talk about coaching and techniques and the merits of this player and that, a place must be found for the joker in the pack. Rugby is meant to be fun and only the crucial eighty minutes should be taken seriously.

Spikey is a conscientious player and a very funny man. On tour he could cause chaos in hotel foyers by imitating accurately the high pitched gurgle of modern telephones. Staff would be scurrying hither and thither looking for the non-existent instrument. Panic set in behind reception desks. Latterly, since joining Newport, his party piece is to mimic the nasal Pontypool drawl of the club coach, Charlie Faulkner. And last year, in the press conference before the French game, when answering a question from a French journalist, he assumed the stilted English of an Inspector Clouseau.

As captain, personality and one-man cabaret (final 't' firmly pronounced), Mike Watkins was exactly the tonic an increasingly introverted Welsh team needed. Now that he has called it a day so prematurely, that much needed twinkle and colour among the grey impersonality will be missed.

22 December

TGRD   Everybody else is on holiday over Christmas but I've got to be out and about. It's a busy time for rugby. Today there are two games, one a schoolboy match and a club match to follow. The first, Wales Schools (Senior section) against New Zealand, was a terrific tussle which Wales won by 12-9. In these stricken times, after the lessons dished out to us by the Aussies, I admit to a sneaking feeling of patriotism, acknowledged last refuge of the scoundrel. It was hard to resist the rising flush of colour around the collar when, very much against the odds, the Welsh boys won. The visitors, after all, had not so much won all their previous matches as blown all opposition out of sight. They had amassed 167 points in their four games and in Wales had scored fifteen tries, while conceding none themselves.

I then negotiated the convoluted series of passage-ways and stairs from the Welsh ground to the Cardiff pitch to see the Cardiff v. Bridgend match. It was not a promising start. The pitch was found to be covered with large areas of surface water of the kind no isolated winger wants to encounter on a cold day. Then there was the matter of the presentation down on the touchline. Stan Bowes, the Cardiff Chairman, stood on the side of the gangway and presented a portrait of Terry Holmes to the great man himself who stood on the other side of the gangway. From underneath the tunnel leading on to the pitch emerged Gareth Williams ahead of the Bridgend team. Very Buster Keaton, he ran straight into the portrait, broke the glass and gashed his knee so badly he had to have five stitches and took no further part in the proceedings. As the whistle blew at last for the start of the game, a Mr. Yule, seasonally enough, was asked for over the loudspeaker system to take an urgent telephone call. Would the festive season now be cancelled?

It turned out to be a very good game which Cardiff won by 34-13.

27 December

TGRD   As a result of yesterday's game against Ponty-pridd, Cardiff's Bob Norster is out with a broken jaw and could be out for two months. He is absolutely essential to any success that is likely to come Wales' way this Home Championship. The only other middle of the line jumper in the squad is Moseley from Pontypool, but he is a bit green as yet at twenty. Where is Waters of Newport? Or Sutton of the South Wales Police? There is no adequate replacement to the position. Will the selectors fall into last year's trap and choose two front of the line players in the line-out as they did, to their cost, against Romania?

6

January

... We are not the first
Who with the best meaning have incurred the worst.
Shakespeare, *King Lear*

5 January

TGRD   It was a startling announcement: Terry Holmes left out of the Welsh squad when the additions were announced last weekend. Who would be a Welsh selector in these anxious times when there are as many opinions over the composition of the National team as there are permutations of the thirty-four players in the squad? But why leave out the one player who might be considered to select himself? Curious thinking.

Could the selectors be showing consideration for a recuperating player not wanting to rush too soon back into the rigours of evening training in the Welsh mid-winter? Yet Paul Thorburn, the young Neath full-back, was promoted to the squad at a time when he was still on the injury list and not likely to be able to play for a week or so. Or would it be unworthy to wonder if they could perhaps be letting the scrum-half know what they felt about his taking a short skiing holiday in Italy at the height of the season? (Gareth Davies, a connoisseur of cold shoulders, had a similar cool reception when he returned after accepting an invitation to play cricket in the Bahamas.) Be that as it may, the effect on the selectors of the furore aroused by Holmes' omission makes me think of Bertie Wooster's Aunt Agatha whose demeanour on a certain occasion "was rather like that of one who, picking the daisies on the railway line, has just caught the down express in the small of the back".

The amazing reason finally given was that since there were three scrum-halves in the squad already, there was no point in including a fourth!

[On Sunday they reconsidered the position and restored Holmes to the squad.]

11 January

TGRD   The announcement of the Welsh team to play France tomorrow week has been delayed until next weekend, no one quite knows why.

The philosophy of squad training seems to be if the patient is ailing, there's nothing so seriously wrong that a spell of squad training cannot put right. If there is no quick recovery, increase the dosage. But who is to say that, sooner or later, the player may not become immune and fail to respond or, more seriously, reject the treatment altogether?

After the Australian game, the Welsh players were called together to discuss the cause of the defeat. Last Sunday the forwards alone were convened and, the following evening, the whole squad practised. Provided that they all survive Saturday's fixtures, there will be a full work-out on the Monday before the team flies to Paris on the Thursday morning. One hopes they will still retain by that stage their appetite for the game at Parc des Princes.

13 January

TGRD   The Welsh selectors announce their team. They make five changes. On his twentieth appearance for Wales Terry Holmes, after originally being excluded from the squad, has now been made the captain. There is one new cap in David Waters of Newport who fills the gap left by Robert Norster, still recovering from the jaw injury against Bridgend before Christmas. Waters had been dropped from the squad but is brought back in the absence of Norster. When they dropped him who else, one wonders, did the selectors have in mind to be the second-string middle-of-the-line jumper? Part of the reason for a squad, surely, is to have the full Welsh team practise together with their shadows.

Billy James comes in for the retired Mike Watkins, and Cardiff's Jeff Whitefoot replaces Ian Stephens of Bridgend at loose-head prop. But – and what a 'but' it is – the combination in the back row, which caused such heated debate last year, remains intact. Richard Moriarty, who missed the last match after he had been sent off (unfairly in my opinion) against Llanelli at Stradey, is recalled after serving his sentence, not at No. 8, as was anticipated and where he has been playing well for Swansea this season, but on the side of the scrum again. The questions which were asked about the balance of this combination still remain. Does it have the strength and weight to be forceful close to the scrum? And has it the ball-winning capacity in the loose?

Malcolm Dacey keeps his position at outside-half although he has not been playing well this season so far. The selectors have preferred to ignore the claims of Gareth Davies who has been playing well all year. To have excluded him again confirms the view that, despite the conciliatory gesture of including him in the squad, he is unlikely to play for Wales during the present coaches' term of office.

One of the Welsh selectors, asked about the controversial position, complained that the media are promoting their own favourites. This is a very negative response. They should be confident of their decision and state clearly why they have chosen Malcolm Dacey as the right man for the job. In this way the player, not to say the public at large, would feel better and more confident. As it is, they are promoting a poor image of themselves, very defensive and, sometimes, stubborn.

17 January

TGRD   Heavy frost covers Europe. Even the fountains in Athens are iced up. So after a week's speculation, France v. Wales, the first match of the Five Nations Championship in Paris, is postponed. This is only the fourth time this has happened since the second world war, and the first time at Parc des Princes, where the ground is frozen to a depth of fifteen centimetres. Albert Ferrasse, President of the FFR, roundly condemned the Paris City Council for their dilatoriness in not covering the pitch in time.

The feeling in Wales is that we should all feel relieved, as France are the outstanding favourites, while the Welsh team gives little confidence to anyone. The match is now put back to 30 March.

At the weekend the Ireland v. England game was also called off.

26 January

TGRD   The Welsh Cup is a great competition and an almost unqualified success. It has generated a massive following and invariably there are memorable matches in the rounds leading up to the final itself which, just as invariably, proves as disappointing as the other rounds are exciting.

It has also managed to put a healthy complexion on many a treasurer's end of season report for those who make progress through and beyond the early rounds. After such expenses as travelling and catering have been paid, the largest sum to be divided between two clubs in the first round this year was £250 with twenty per cent of that going into the Competition Reserve Fund. It is from the quarter-final stage onwards that the financial benefit begins to accrue. In the penultimate round the four clubs get fifteen per cent of the pooled receipts of the two games played on neutral grounds, with the fund and the host clubs also getting a percentage share. The finalists receive thirty per cent, up to a maximum £12,000 of the gate takings at the Arms Park, with the fund and the WRU being the other beneficiaries.

There have been murmurings of late that increasingly the major share of the Cup revenue goes into the pocket of the few and in financial terms is beginning to create an elite of prosperous clubs. A look at the figures for the thirteen-year history of the competition may confirm the view.

Llanelli, Cardiff and Bridgend between them have won the Cup nine times, have been losing finalists five times and semi-finalists on another nine separate occasions. Neath, Newport, Pontypool and Swansea have been the other winners. Apart from Aberavon, who have been six times semi-finalists, there is a fairly even distribution of placings among the other eleven clubs who have, at some time or other, reached the semi-final stage. Seven of the so-called senior clubs have never gone that far: Abertillery, Cross Keys, Glamorgan Wanderers, Maesteg, Penarth, South Wales Police and Tredegar.

While it could be argued that excellence is rewarded, the danger is that, if the trend continues, the base from which that excellence emerges might become too narrow. Players will be drawn to those clubs whose winning windfalls allow them better facilities.

For the time being, however, Ray Williams, the WRU Secretary, does not envisage a change of financial policy. Though little money is generated to clubs knocked out in the early rounds, the WRU does grant the first five units of insurance for each club in Wales out of its reserve, and there are 943 of them.

Proceeds from the Cup competition also form part of a grand design. Since the Schweppes Cup is self-financing, the sponsorship money, about £150,000 over each period of three years (but liable to tax), has gone towards the £10,000,000 ground development. The debt is expected to be cleared by the end of the decade, an achievement which the other nations may look on with envy. The WRU will then be, as they say, in a profit-making situation. By that time each home match at the Arms Park will generate revenue of half a million pounds. The question then, and a crucial one too, will be what is to happen to that revenue, large by any standards, and a considerable resource in an amateur game?

26 January

JM What a big day for the Forest of Dean. Lydney were travelling to Redruth in the third round of the John Player Cup: would they reach the fourth for the first time ever? A special train had been hired and sold out. More exciting though was the away match between Berry Hill, a club equidistant from my house as Lydney, and Bath, the Cup-holders and the favourites to win again. I decide to go along with Berry Hill.

Unfreezing the lock on the car, I set off through the Forest on a sunlit morning. On the radio at ten o'clock I hear that a colleague with whom I had helped set up Harlech Television, David, Lord Harlech, had been killed in a car accident in North Wales. I wondered, being so shocked, whether to call off the Bath excursion. So many memories came back at once and were to continue to do so during the day, of the excitement of our plan, our day together at the IBA before Lord Hill, the news of winning and the pleasure of the creation of the television station. His elegance, charm and, to me, kindness, were to trouble the day. One of his favourite phrases at board meetings was: "Shall we kick to touch this time?" I drove on.

The Berry Hill club has come up in the world. It has floodlights, six teams, two youth teams. There is a real ambition in this small community to become a first-class club playing the more celebrated. The name Berry Hill is not arboreal but derives from the fact that, before the coal mines came and went, this was an ancient burial ground. This, as much else, I learned from John Belcher, the Press Secretary, an art teacher at a local school who played a lot of rugby himself and who has designed many club badges in the district. He also writes – an important propaganda function this for rugby clubs – the reports of matches for the local press. He was not, however, responsible for a famous report of a victory for Berry Hill on a cheerful tour when the match had been lost. That had been the work of an enterprising player in much the condition when he telephoned as he had been on the field at the end of an interesting few matches near Newcastle.

John introduced me to his Chairman, Kevin Horrabin, a manager at the Rank Xerox works nearby, and to the Baldwin family: John was the Secretary, Kevin the Treasurer. Their father had been the Secretary for many years, a nephew was playing at No. 8 in the team. I was told as we waited for the bus to take us to Bath and the high rugby life, that at Berry Hill there was no special bar for the first team. All mixed together. On the other hand, there were clubs in the Forest of Dean where a segregation did exist, especially clubs richer than Berry Hill which were perhaps more social clubs than rugby clubs. I sensed that rivalry was strong.

When I set off with the team in their coach, I realised that there were seven other coaches of supporters following us. Many from the village were travelling by car. "What a great day," said someone, "for any burglars in Berry Hill. Everyone will be in Bath." We drove down the Wye Valley in the sun and across the Severn Bridge and drew up at a posh pub called The Compass at Tormanton. It was very county, the players thought. They were impressed that at 95p a pint, drinks were 30p more than at their rugby club. We had a good buffet lunch which the players did not have to pay for and left in high spirits for the match.

The sun was still shining and Bath looked, as ever, very beautiful around the rugby ground. In the dressing room the Berry Hill team were cheerful. They didn't expect to win but intended to enjoy themselves. They were curious to see how they would do against a team fielding nine English Internationals. Suddenly a stranger could realise quite what a valuable exercise this Cup tourney was and yet I had learned that it was the case that several of the men playing for Berry Hill could themselves be playing for teams like Gloucester or Bristol or, given Bath's policy of finding players far from Beau Brummel's town, even their opponents of the day. The Berry Hill players of high quality prefer to play for their local club. They hope to help it reach a higher status. They also like the life and fun of the club. Their loyalty, of course, diminishes their chances of attracting the attention that might win them a place in or near the English National team. Oddly, to a Welshman, this does not seem to trouble them as much as it might. There are more serious reasons for unease in English rugby, but the aspirations of local clubs and the attitudes of players may be, if minor, relevant among them.

The Berry Hill supporters made far more noise than Bath's during the match. "Here we go, here we go, here we go," they cried. There must have been some 7,000 Bath supporters, some 750 Berry Hill. Over the loud-speaker spectators were asked if they would mind standing behind rather than in front of advertising hoardings. HTV's cameras were present and, clearly, those helping pay for affairs did not want their signs obscured. Bath won by twenty-four points to a penalty goal, but Berry Hill came close to scoring a try twice. I thought I would

77

wait for John Belcher's account of the match in next week's *Forest of Dean Guardian*.

In the club house the contrast between the character of the Bath and the Berry Hill supporters could be taken as an illumination of British social life as much as rugby life. On the one hand, here was the essence of middle-, even upper-class rugby; on the other the working class. But as the evening gathered strength more subtle elements came into the contrast. There was gossip, of course, as there is at Wasps and London Welsh, about how it is that certain clubs in England manage to gather together so many gifted players who live, or once lived, so far from the club. What inducements are offered? To be fair, there is the same gossip in West Wales.

John Horton, the Bath and English outside-half, was in his, as I gathered, usual good form and spent much time with the Berry Hill team. I hadn't realised that he had played in France from time to time. There were some mysterious transactions taking place which efforts were being made to conceal. It seemed the players were not happy that they were not *all* allowed to drink in the room reserved for the sponsors and their guests. I concluded that the usual rugby players' revenge was being taken and that drink was being removed from somewhere. I was told that other clubs' players had also objected to this practice by the sponsors: who, they properly wished to know, had the spectators come to see?

By this time – 7.30 – I had begun to realise that I had some eight miles to drive from the Berry Hill club house when we returned and thought I had best aim for sobriety. In the Bath club house there was a television set. On it there appeared the great pianist Alfred Brendel and who should be with him but one of the finest of all lieder singers, Dietrich Fischer-Dieskau. They were to sing Schubert's *Winterreise*. I turned up the sound. In the uproar of the bar no one noticed. One of the Berry Hill supporters sat alongside me and talked about his father's role in the Labour party in the Forest of Dean a long time ago.

This peculiar isolation did not last since a debate broke out which I take to be characteristic of John Player Cup matches between the great and the aspiring. Several of the Berry Hill supporters, quite how many was not clear, had chosen to miss their bus home. Therefore they wanted to travel on the players' bus. But, the argument went, if all the players came on the bus, then there would be no room for these stray supporters. At this point several players said they did not want to go home on the bus. They argued that since they had been playing, were they not entitled to taxis home? Why could they not enjoy Bath a little longer than ten o'clock?

Exhibiting great tact, it seemed to me, the Berry Hill powers solved the problem swiftly. The supporters would come on the bus; those players that wished them would have taxis. And so we set off in the bus, calling at a chip shop here, a Chinese take-away there, everyone happy. Back at the Berry Hill club house we discovered my car frozen, but with matches and cigarette lighters we unfroze the locks and cleared the windscreen. I drove a few people home and arrived myself in snow at one o'clock in the morning.

28 January

JM   *The Times* writes that Berry Hill would have beaten some of the other teams in the third round of the John Player Cup. It was their ill luck to have run up against Bath, but given the occasion, the greatest in their ninety-six-year-old history, they probably played above themselves. Watch out for them, he writes, next year.

7

February

What men call social virtues, good fellowship, is commonly but the virtue of pigs in a litter, which lie close together to keep each other warm. It brings men together in crowds and mobs in bar-rooms and elsewhere, but it does not deserve the name of virtue.

Thoreau

1 February

JM   John Belcher's account of the match appears in the local *Guardian*:

Berry Hill fought hard throughout the game to overcome the cup holders, but the power of the Bath three-quarters, coupled with some inept refereeing, eventually sealed their fate. The Berry Hill pack continuously out-scrummaged their illustrious opponents but were frustrated by their illegal tactics of collapsing the scrum every time they were under pressure – tactics that went unpunished by the referee even though it was patently obvious to practically all those present with any knowledge of rugby. Ironically Bath had taken the lead with a penalty by full-back John Palmer after the referee had penalised Berry Hill for collapsing the scrum on their own 22-metre line.

So [he concluded after a fair account of the match] Berry Hill are out of the Cup but they played rugby far above the standard of their so-called 'junior' status and won extravagant praise from a team that contained nine Internationals and is reported to have the fastest back division in Britain.

In the Berry Hill team, although scrum-half B. Richards was the only Welshman, seven others, exhibit-

GREN.

"I SEE GERALD'S BEEN OUT FOR A RUN!"

M, seen here leading Swansea Grammar School, was often the captain of the team, since he
as too boring a player otherwise to hold his place. He also kicked the goals.

Early rounds: **above** a John Player Cup tie between the Forest of Dean club Lydney and fashionable Sale (in the hoops) disturbed preconceptions about Gloucestershire rugby. Lydney, who lost at home, played an open game. The sun shone. There was no rough play. Only cynics put this last down to the presence of the television cameras. **Below,** Risca entertain Llanelli in the second round of the Schweppes Cup. Here Gary Pearce makes a contribution to the Scarlets' comfortable score line, as he was to clinch the one point difference in the final against Cardiff.

As one would expect from a speech-writer to Malcolm Fraser, former Australian Prime Minister, coach Alan Jones **above** was knowledgeable and articulate. He knew the value of public relations and the art of communication. ''One day you can be the rooster and the next the feather duster,'' he said after his team had beaten Wales and only Scotland stood betwen them and a Grand Slam.

As well as knowing the art of coaching, Ireland's Mick Doyle also understands the virtue of doing it with a smile. His insouciant style was in marked contrast to the grim approach of others. Here **left** he scents the wind of an Irish championship with Tom Kiernan and Syd Millar.

Mark Ring: Welsh rugby's player of the year. Among the disciplined roundheads alongside him, here was an adventurous cavalier who added colour to an otherwise grey Welsh seas: A star performer, he stood apart from the drab uniformity that much of coaching appears to promote. **Above**, running free against the Barbarians; **below**, scoring for Cardiff against Pontypool in the semi-final of the Schweppes Cup.

Holmes is where the heart is. Wales, if they were to stand any chance in the championship, needed Terry Holmes at the core of the side. For most of the time too much was asked of him. **Above**, brought down short of the Newbridge line, he still gets in his pass. **Below**, against England he was for the first time relieved of the burden of shoring up the Welsh back row, and freed to act out his role as scrum-half successfully.

Serge Blanco, the French full-back, enlivened the season with his speed and brilliance of his judgement in entering the three-quarter line. Against Scotland and Wales he seemed to breach defences at will.

Patrick Estève, for all that he scored fine tries against Ireland and Wales, will be remembered as the wing who made the match against England a draw at Twickenham instead of a victory for France, when he was tackled in possession behind the try line. All tackles must now have an extra haunting quality for him.

bove, despite the discrepancy in height, Robert Norster at 6ft 4ins dominated the line-out
ainst England's Preston Grasshopper, Wade Dooley, 6ft 8ins. Norster, of all forwards, ought
have the protective cover once reserved for outside halves. **Below**, he keeps on his feet as
nelli come at him from all sides in the Schweppes Cup Final.

Final reckonings: **above**, Bath, in white, were always the favourites for the John Player Cup but London Welsh came back from sixteen points down at half time to contest an exciting second half. **Below**, The WRU dream — a final between Cardiff and Llanelli in the Schwepp Cup. But this time the favourites, Cardiff, lost by a bootlace. Llanelli scrum-half Jonathan Griffiths, comes up to take a scoring pass from Martin Gravelle.

ing the traffic over the border in the past coal-mining century, had Welsh surnames: J. Powell, S. Powell, R. Morgan, R. Lewis, P. Price, B. K. Harris, J. Evans.

Lydney beat Redruth with ease and are to play Sale in the next round, a draw which three years ago was not a pleasant encounter.

1–2 February

TGRD   Loitering on the steps of the North British Hotel in Edinburgh, as an aimless Welshman before the Scottish v. Irish game, I caught up with Mick Doyle for the first time since 1968 when we had shared many a room together on a Lions tour. We had a brief exchange, so brief it was a downright insult to all those intervening years. But he had a rendezvous with the players so there was no time to dilly-dally.

He is a coach after my own heart, with a glint of a mischievous glimmer in his eye. He actually looks as if he might be enjoying himself. He might not even take it too seriously. It is all very Irish and laid back. He does not wear a hang-dog, careworn look of a coach who assumes all the problems of the rugby-playing world. Nor does he hang around and talk as if everyone ought to believe he has all the answers. If he has ambition it is not at all obvious. In that brief encounter he had time to say that if his team did not play a running game or at least attempt to do so, then coaching held little charm for him.

The following morning I bump into him again, and I wonder whether any Welsh coach would have the disinterestedness, lack of conceit and the foresight to do what Mick Doyle says he did to motivate his team on the evening before the game. Or was Mick pulling my leg? "Last night," he said, "I showed a video of the Welsh performances in the 'seventies. It was meant to inspire. I just let them relax and watch it." And at the end? "Well, I

81

told them that if those buggers from Wales could play like that, then so could they!"

And on the day itself they went out and went a long way to achieving what their coach had promised.

The recent Australians – and their memory is going to gnaw away at us for the rest of the season – served to remind us of what our own virtues once were, which we have allowed ourselves to forget. Their play showed that there is more to good rugby than scrummaging (and they outshone Wales even here), playing the percentage game and kicking penalties. Mick Doyle acknowledges the debt.

"There is no recognised kicker in our team," he said after the match in which he had seen Kiernan miss three kickable penalties in the first half. "If that is the case, so be it. I shall not worry. If the only option a team has is to kick goals, and that fails, then it jolts the team's morale to see them missed. There have to be other options."

This was not the confident blarney of a coach who has seen his team win, because he had been saying exactly this before the game began. Their intention had been adventure, and they assuredly laid to rest the old joke, "Kick ahead, Ireland. Kick ahead. Any bloody head!"

In the grand manner of all the ambitious talk beforehand Ireland started with a flourish. They could have brought about a devastating score in the first minute but didn't. But there was no misfortune in the final minute when with audacious inventiveness and a superlative piece of attacking rugby the three-quarters brought off a brilliant try to come from behind and win the game in thrilling fashion.

If no one else is on the right lines in this country, then Mick Doyle is.

Robert Norster is due to return tomorrow after having been out of the game since 22 December. Whilst this will be of considerable relief to all who have the best interests of the Welsh team at heart, it will be nothing short of wretched news to David Waters who had been selected to play in the match, now postponed, against France. Although he has played for Wales B, the final accolade may elude him.

In Welsh terms Norster, of all forwards, ought to have protection cover of the kind once reserved only for outside-halves. Never considered one of the elite in a way that even front-row forwards sometimes are, the tall middle-of-the-line jumper is a rare breed to be valued. Even a cursory glance at hereditary patterns suggests that Wales is never going to be awash with such men. Norster's well-being is almost as crucial to the Welsh team as Holmes' on whose shoulders, literally, a lot will depend. Dintrans, the French captain, in expressing his disappointment that the encounter with Wales was called off, referred not only to the controversial decision at outside-half but also to Norster's recovery, which he saw as posing a considerable threat. France for all their undoubted gifts are unsure of their locks. Norster has been an automatic choice since his first cap against Scotland in 1982, but in the event of his enforced absence no adequate replacement has been found.

By assidious application, the mechanics of the scrum can be mastered by physically smaller men, as the Japanese have assuredly done, but however many stratagems they may have up their sleeves, nothing will compensate for lack of height in the line-out, and no amount of rigorous training and discipline can rectify this. The very tall man is a prerequisite in the middle of the line-out. I'm not certain that this lesson has been learnt yet, particularly in view of the fact that for the game against Romania last season Wales took two front-of-the-line jumpers and ignored the need for a specialist in the other lock position.

In this respect it is surprising that Steve Sutton, capped by Wales in 1982 before Norster came along, and standing at 6 ft 5 ins, should have been demoted so quickly at the end of that season, and left out in the cold since then. The reason given at the time – in Romania, in fact, after the weakness had been exposed – was that Sutton had failed to show the necessary mettle and fortitude in fulfilling the mechanical tests and measurements which the Welsh team underwent at the time. He was said not to be motivated by the stop watch and, putting a sinister twist on the age of advancing high-tech, he allowed the machines to get the better of him. He showed too human qualities and gave in when the going got too tough for his own well-being.

This was a strangely misguided appliance of science to a team game which also measures itself by a special chemistry of interaction and personality. Neither the machine nor the stop watch can quantify this, but a clever and understanding coach can, through guidance and persuasion. Coaching is as much a matter of coaching and preparing the mind as it is about the teaching of techniques and physical skills; it is about the occasional use of the lashing word, as it is of the honeyed tongue. Tests and measurements have their place, but not in isolation from the many other aspects which make up the profile of a good team.

So Sutton has been sacrificed at this particular altar of the new more scientific thinking. As a result Wales are short of a tall middle-of-the-line jumper.

2 February

JM England play France at Twickenham. This match belonged to Patrick Estève, the French wing three-quarter. England began with an exuberance which suggested that the tedium of the victory over Romania earlier in the season was to be replaced with life, even pleasure. The Cambridge outside-half, C. R. Andrew, had the look, if it does not sound too patronising, of a Welsh outside-half, like an earlier one from Cambridge,

Glyn Davies. That composed air of the natural games player, that sense of intelligence, was immediately to be recognised. What a pity then that referee and linesmen weren't sharper at seeing a bad and then a worse late tackle on him by the French back row. Each was bound to put him a little off his game. The balance of a match can so easily be unfairly spoiled.

Although I had been to Twickenham often before to watch Wales play England, I had never seen England play another nation. The men and women sitting in the stand around me did not appear to know the rules of rugby football; some, it struck me, had never seen a match before. What is happening now? they would ask their neighbours, who didn't know either. You had the sense of being among American tourists expecting Noël Coward who had fetched up at a National Theatre production of *Coriolanus* by mistake. The singing of 'Land of Hope and Glory', however, was rousing. I recalled a phrase I had used in the 'fifties writing about 'Twickers': here was the *lumpenbourgeoisie* at play.

The French team slowly came into the game, although looking a little bad tempered. Their defensive play was matchless. When they began to attack they made a perfect break through the English defence and the left wing, Estève, took a pass from his brilliant centre, Sella, and crossed the line. Instead of touching the ball down for a try which would, as it turned out, have won the match, he ran towards the posts. The English scrum-half Richard Harding kept on chasing – he must have run fifty yards in pursuit of the French three-quarters – and he caught the Frenchman and prevented the try being scored. Harding was, very properly, the hero of the hour: it is Estève who will be remembered for ever.

The drawn match was held to have been a triumph for England I gathered, mooching through the west car park after the match. My son, who had driven us there in a battered Renault 5 he is trying to hold together, sometimes with string, was taken aback to see such a collection of Rolls-Royces, Jaguars, Alfa Romeos and Volvos, each with its hampers and champagne. Surely, England cannot be quite the European poor relation when this cornucopia is offered, was the sort of remark we were working towards.

Driving away I noted how many wives, or women, were driving Rolls-Royces occupied by husbands, or men of some status. This would not have happened in the 'fifties or early 'sixties. The idea then that a macho rugby man would allow his wife to drive his Rolls would have been as improbable as men in the Dark Ages believing the world was other than flat. The man who is now macho at the bar cannot be behind the wheel. Therefore the woman has to stay sober. When Mrs. Barbara Castle in the 1966 Labour Cabinet invented the breathalyser, can she have anticipated so bizarre a form both of women's liberation and a chore? In this field of play, as in so many others, it scarcely seems an advance of the female cause: the new status at the wheel requires an abnegation of the old freedom to the champagne. What strange paradoxes life holds, we agreed. One other piece of research was odd. It took exactly the length of time to drive from our flat in Swiss Cottage to Twickenham – a distance of twelve miles – as it takes to drive to Cardiff Arms Park from our house on the Welsh border – a distance of forty-eight miles.

9 February

TGRD   Snow. Matches off all over Wales. When the snow comes to our village there is absolute stillness and silence. Nothing stirs. No traffic or animal noises. The village is cut off completely. To all points of the compass there are hills and slopes which are suddenly transformed into Alpine toboggan tracks or, to the sophisticates of the village, ski-runs. This will provide a diversion but, after the first interlude three weeks ago, an unwelcome one now, as it breaks up the rhythm and the style of the season. No matches to report. There is a strong sense of detachment. Life can and does go on every Saturday. Yet, if this carries on for very much longer I'll begin suffering withdrawal symptoms. Could I do without this weekly fix? Is there life after Rugby Football?

Of course, it is perfectly possible to live in Wales and not be touched by rugby football. After all, Wales with its radical, non-conformist tradition has always appealed as a refuge for minority groups, and has always liked to believe that it encourages those with alternative ways of thinking and behaving. It is possible to fain innocence of the game's mysteries or claim ignorance of its great, almost masonic, influence in this part of the world. A man, suffering some strange disorder, may simply declare a personal lack of comprehension. But, at his peril, should he affect such disdain as to dismiss rugby as beneath general consideration. Such a man would be well advised to take a long boat trip to the South China Seas or to choose his eight discs and disappear to a desert island of his choice, rather than persist in living in the principality. For like it or not, sooner or later, he will be waylaid like Coleridge's Wedding Guest by some grey-beard loon with glittering eye determined to air his own version of the ills which currently beset the Welsh National team. The Ancient Supporter will boil with rage and go puce in the face, these disturbing aspects only subsiding when he shifts his ground and begins reliving his childhood recollection of the rugby heroes of his past, becalmed now in a wave of warm, over-baked nostalgia.

For an outsider, such intoxication is difficult to understand. We, in Wales, are moved to make extravagant claims for a game which is often inelegant and tantalisingly flawed. The game's laws are full of strange mysteries; reputedly a handling game, the ball is kicked more often than not; in a passing game to kick the ball *out* of play is part of the cunning tactical plan. The ball is in play for half the duration of the match and curiously intricate ploys are so arranged that clutches of bodies end up in graceless heaps. But in such inconsistencies reside its eternal fascination and frustration.

The past is always present in rugby, especially in Wales, and the present Welsh team suffer in the stretching shadow of the 'seventies. The only bit of cork in that champagne period was that the All Blacks retained their international superiority at the Arms Park. On the ground we venerate as a shrine, and they briskly refer to as the paddock, they reduced our mystical pretensions.

For all that the Arms Park (forget the grey monolithic words National Stadium) is a congregational gathering, an *eisteddfod* where the north and south of Wales, the English and the Welsh languages meet to watch a game in a language everyone understands – except, they will all agree, the referee.

And it was a referee who was at the centre of that muffled, ambiguous moment in 1905 that established the game in the Welsh mythology. Bob Deans of New Zealand claimed to have scored a try. Rhys Gabe and Teddy Morgan of Wales argued that he did not. The referee on this occasion sided with the Welshmen who won a famous victory. Most observers at the time were mystified by what was supposed to have happened. But that moment, so full of doubt on the day, has attained a remarkable clarity ever since. No such doubt exists nowadays. All New Zealanders, from their nappy days onwards, know Deans scored. Every Welshman born begs vehemently to differ. Since that December day the status of the game has been securely assured. It can spread an infectious excitement and joy as well as provoke a stifling prejudice and introversion. It can bring a voluble nation to silence or, more easily, prompt it to sing in celebration.

The rugby coach of today has yet to come to terms with this chemistry and what embodies it – the idiosyncrasies of the talented player. Yet without the star performance, without the flash of an individual genius, rugby can decline into a bruising confrontation. And for a Welshman the game is real only if tinged with elements of dazzling fantasy.

9 February

JM   Snowed in. To have two foot of snow in the garden and outside the front door is delightful, there is no doubt about it. But there is no rugby. The farmer next door, across the ford, has a vehicle which can conquer snow, ice or whatever, and so we drove, spinning from time to time, up the hill. We went off the road once. We collected a few friends and one young girl grew frightened as we spun. I reflected on how miserable I used to be when young when matches were called off because of frost and snow. With what sweet enthusiasm we used to go to the school or village ground, and so much want to play. This was to have been Gerald's fortieth birthday party across the river, but he, too, was snowed in.

10 February

JM   Snowed in another day, I began to brood on the condition of rugby in Britain after the Australian tour. I have always believed there is a relationship between the state of a nation's economy and the flowering of the National team, at least in Wales. Carwyn James, good *Plaidwr* that he was, disputed my correlation of the success of Barry John with the financial boom of the Heath government, but was mollified when I quoted Hegel at him. Hegel, seeing Napoleon at the Battle of Jena, said that he had not simply seen the revolutionary soldier: he had seen 'an idea on horseback'. Carwyn liked that.

The problem of rugby now, in England as much as in Wales, is that it still mirrors the problems of the economy, but differently. The trouble with Britain is management. The mediocre cling to their jobs. More, they ensure that their juniors are sufficiently mediocre not to threaten them. In the United States, managers are required to find bright inheritors: in Britain not so. Worse, in Britain, in industry as in rugby, talent is feared, the eccentric abhorred, the mischief-making dancer a man to be watched for, someone who will rock the boat. The boat needs to be rocked.

14 February

JM The match between Wales and England was called off today. For all the hard work at the Arms Park – and we still prefer that name to the National Stadium – the ground was too hard. It will probably be played in late April depending on the demands of various Cup competitions. There is much to be said for playing International matches later in the season. The players might have more chance to play, not be so much at the mercy of cold and wind, although, of course, the elements are part of the test in rugby, as in battle: they tax the wits more.

16 February

JM A crisp winter day on this side of the river. Perhaps the England game could have been played after all? Instead I go three miles up the hill to see a match which could not have been more removed from the scene of National glamour.

Bream is one of those Forest of Dean rugby clubs which show small interest in matters elsewhere. It has nearly a thousand social club members, some 140 rugby members. It costs a pound a year to belong. Housed in an old Miners' Welfare Hall and cinema, its comforts are great.

So I strolled down the hill to the field where the third team were playing a Gloucester City suburban team. The playing field is held to slope more than any other in England and I could believe it. By some Welsh standards it was flat. To my left the abundant trees of the Forest were not yet in leaf: away to the west I could see the land rise where Wales asserts itself. There were ten spectators, all to do with the club, selectors, helpers with corner flags.

I learned that the team's leading lights were in the north of England on tour for the weekend. Tours tend to be made up of players who fancy or can afford a trip rather than those whose skill might be more sportingly appraised. I applied my attention to matters in hand.

Why, I asked rather diffidently, is there so much fighting? Why is the referee having such a hard time? Is it always like this? The visiting captain had shouted to the referee that he was going to report him to the Gloucester Union. No, no, they said, it is seldom like this. There is a special reason. The year before the Bream team had sent its thirds to play in Gloucester against today's rivals; the latter had played their first team. Bream had thus lost by a century of points. They didn't care for this. Today therefore was a brisk riposte. It certainly was.

Wives and mothers and girl friends of members were making meals in the club house after the match. The air between the two teams was some ten yards, the feeling, I sensed, uneasy. I learned that the captain had formally told the referee that he was going to complain. The referee responded that he was quite entitled to tell a forward not involved in a fight that was spontaneous, that he should not arrive later to join in. This seemed a fair point. In the bar a club member asked the Chairman if it was in order to conduct a raffle for the benefit of one of their number whose wife had just been killed in a car accident. The decision was favourable and the raffle was held.

JM   Don Llewellyn of HTV Wales who is to direct a television film which will accompany our book calls to begin discussions on a style we might adopt.

Since the object of the film is to discover what rugby players have in common in different social classes and nations, we wanted to see the detail of club life; indeed concentrate more on the humbler teams than on the grand or International performers. We would consider one match in detail, Don proposing that we try to cover the game from behind the goal posts. This angle he believes offers a clearer idea of the development of a move and permits an audience to gain an insight into vital elements in the angle of running a three-quarter adopts. The technique, for example, of the fine French full-back, Blanco, and the manner in which he enters the three-quarter line is more acutely appreciated when viewed from behind the try line.

JM   What is it, Don and I wonder, that gives rugby players a passion for stealing furniture from pubs and hotels? He talked about a trip his team Pentyrch, near Cardiff, made to North Wales for a 'missionary' game in that largely uncharted and unconverted territory. The players ate a meal in a hotel after the match. Many took mementoes back to the charabanc. Don, being captain of Pentyrch – he was to break his neck hooking for them – counted his comrades and found one missing. No one was quite sober, but they could still count. They returned to the hotel to search. The missing player could not be found. As they were about to leave the hallway they heard a movement at the head of the stairs. A suit of armour moved, slipped and tumbled down, crashing at their feet. Their friend had been trying to make away with it, and is still known as the Black Knight.

I responded with an account of a match between University Colleges Swansea – where I was in my first week as an undergraduate – and Cardiff at the latter's ground. Our team was composed mainly of ex-servicemen (this was 1947), many of them war heroes. Since I was only seventeen, I held them in awe. They were hard-drinking men. Many were to play for the Swansea club while at university.

After the game we drank in a hotel or, rather, they did, since I was an abstainer in those innocent days. When the bar closed my colleagues removed the furniture from the pub and placed it – I recall a hat stand, a table with chairs placed around it, several plaques – on the lawn outside. The proprietor sent for the police and those of us slow enough to be hanging around were taken to the police station and put in the cells. The police took some of the furniture as evidence. Some members of the team who had not been arrested then managed to come into the police station, steal the hat stand and a chair once more and place them outside Cardiff's grand City Hall. This coup so astonished the authorities that we were released from jail without being charged. When I returned home in the middle of the night my parents, who had been so proud that I had won a scholarship to the university, were shocked that it should have led to the cooler in Cardiff. But my grandmother said that in her day rugby players were often in jail for fighting and drinking. At the turn of the century the game was known among the God-fearing as 'the twin sister of the drinking system'.

23 February

JM   What an unpredictable match this has turned out to be, the fourth round John Player Cup tie between Lydney and Sale. The snow has cleared. There has been no rugby for three weeks, and so there was an expectation that the ground would be sodden. More than that, there was a fear that there would be a rerun of a tough match here between Lydney and Sale in the Cup three years ago. This day the sun shone. The ground was firm. The match was played in such a clean, even elegant, way that those familiar with Lydney's repute as a hard side were puzzled. Cynics put it down to the fact that television cameras were present and so the locals wished to behave themselves. I think that an unfair judgement. More likely the Lydney coach, John Haines, who played for Gloucester for fifteen years, is reflecting a dramatic change in Gloucestershire rugby: the boys are running the ball. Sale won comfortably, their backs being that bit sharper, just.

Lydney had men who had played for Gloucester, Bristol and Pontypool. The club's programme notes are entertaining: "Jeremy Weech (lock): earns a living catching salmon in the Highlands of Scotland in the summer and as an unpaid lock for Lydney in the winter. Jeremy gets better as the years go by. He lists his hobbies as playing pool and milking cows."

In the gents at half time there were jokes about AIDS, the affliction being the subject of newspaper scare stories this week. A supporter complained that he had missed two tries by being in the lavatory. "Why," asked a neighbour, "don't you try sticking it in your ear like the rest of us?"

24 February

JM   We drove along the Wye Valley to Monmouth and then across the Usk to Gerald's fortieth birthday party which had been postponed for a fortnight because so many of us were snowed in. His house commands a view of unexpected beauty: this part of Gwent is hardly known to strangers, the hills gentle and green, a territory lost between Pontypool and Usk town. My son Aled who is twenty-one and hasn't missed a Home International at the Arms Park since he was eight years old, came with us and was to drive us home, not being a drinking boy. What a pleasure to know that it would be possible to drink as much champagne as was offered. Much was. Indeed I took along a bottle from one of the few vineyards in France owned by a woman, a fact which could be milked for jokes, to wit: a little on the sharp side, or full of promise, or needs a little ageing. Another present we took was the *Oxford Book of Narrative Verse*. Aled noted that even the estate agent's sign on a board across the road from the house was in the shape of a rugby ball.

Barry John arrived, shook his host by the hand and said, "So glad you could come." I had met him and Gerald first in South Africa in 1968 when they were playing for the British Lions. Barry impressed me by his achievement in managing to stay throughout the tour, even though he had broken his collar bone in the First Test and did not play another match. A young man, I thought, who could achieve this unique feat, who could so charm the management, would go far. I decided that when they returned to Wales I would try and make a television film for Harlech TV about the pair of dazzling players. It was made and was to contain one of the most remarkable displays by Barry that any sportsman can have offered – certainly for the record.

The Welsh Rugby Union gave us permission for the outside-half to wear a microphone during a match between Cardiff and Swansea at the Arms Park. The audience would thus feel itself part of the game and hear the Cardiff star's chat: he only swore once. The crew and I and the director, Jolyon Wimhurst, stood on the touch-line. From time to time Barry would come and talk, even though this was a serious match between two of the most powerful rival clubs in Britain. What would we like him to do? Not believing that he could be serious, I asked if he would mind scoring a try at the corner flag at the City end of the ground. We positioned ourselves there. Within five minutes he not only had scored a try there, but had wilfully, smiling a little, chosen to jink and glide past seven Swansea players in scoring it. And so it went on. Would we like him to drop a goal? He did. What about kicking a penalty goal? At that time he was not the principal goal kicker for Cardiff or, oddly enough, for Wales. However, he asked his captain if he could have the next kick at goal: certainly. He kicked it. I doubt if anyone else on the field knew what he was doing. Indeed I doubt if the Swansea team would have been best pleased to learn that here was the Cardiff outside-half scoring cheerfully whenever it suited him, for all his opponents' efforts.

His style has not changed. He told us of how in the famous Grand Slam match in Paris in 1971, John Taylor had said to him in the tunnel as they ran on to the field at Stades Colombes: "Barry, this is a serious match." What could this mean? "It means you are tackling today." Barry ran to the captain, John Dawes, and complained: "I'm not playing; tackling isn't in my contract." In that match he broke his nose making a tackle that helped win the Grand Slam and subsequently wondered who it was that had pushed him. He maintains that he never had any mud on any of his Welsh jerseys, and who would dispute it?

Many of that wonderful Welsh side, the best since the turn of the century, remain friends and see much of each other, especially since so many of them are commentators on the game, whether for newspapers or the broadcasting companies. It was a gifted generation. Unlike too many more recent players, they still laugh a lot and did at the party.

8

March

The creative mind is a flower in search of its natural air of unconditioned freedom. It can perish at any moment from the crude blades and stifling hoods of bigoted authority.

Gwyn Thomas

1 March

TGRD Eddie Butler's abrupt announcement that he is retiring from International rugby is the latest in a disquieting trend. Two years ago, his colleagues in Pontypool, Jeff Squire and Graham Price, also retired among rumours of disillusionment with rugby at the highest level, and earlier this season, Mike Watkins, last year's popular captain, who partly revived Welsh performances in the Five Nations Championship, made a similar statement. It is curious, in Butler's case, after being selected for the two postponed games against France and England, to have chosen the third occasion to call it a day. This has increased the suspicion that all is not well within the Welsh squad. For his part Butler has firmly refused to comment on such speculation. His pronouncement, however, indicates a genuine sense of unhappiness, not so much with the Welsh squad, but rather with external pressures in the form of very personalised criticism and, in some cases, almost vindictive condemnation. After two years of it, he has finally found it unbearable and harmful to his own peace of mind.

The vociferous public disapproval of the Welsh team has almost become personalised in his name. The disquieting feature is that after being fed on the excesses of the 'seventies there is an element of the public unable to come to grips with anything less than automatic success.

97

It is no exaggeration to say that Butler has taken the brunt of the accusations.

Playing for Pontypool he has proved himself to be the best No. 8 currently playing in Wales. To suggest that he is no Mervyn Davies, who is still the best No. 8 Wales has ever had, is missing the point altogether and is to be regretted. If he had continued to be supported on the International field by a blind-side flanker in the mould of Jeff Squire, more able to assist in carrying out the chores close to the scrum, there would have been a better balance to the back row as a whole.

However Butler's dilemma raises a fundamental point about the nature of the game and our attitudes to it. Increasingly in terms of training and preparation and the exposure it gets it has begun to resemble a professional sport. But since it remains an amateur game, should the demands we make of it be the same? After all, once the game is over, there is the more serious business of earning a living. Whatever the appearances are to the contrary, he is not a paid entertainer and an amateur rugby player, unlike his professional counterpart, cannot suffer the slings and arrows of outrageous criticism and look to his bank balance for compensation.

"Nice guys don't win," someone remarked. But it is a sad day when such a tired, cynical axiom should have to be resurrected for a man who plays rugby for the genuine love of it. As to those who have been prompted to write him venomous anonymous notes, Eddie Butler, in quieter moments, might like to reflect that at least he is among the few who have had the enormous satisfaction on sixteen occasions of wearing the red jersey of Wales, to which those with the ready pen cannot possibly hope to aspire.

2 March

JM   The plan, honest, was to fly to Dublin from Cardiff to watch Ireland play France. The Irish were in a new and exciting spirit: France were determined to win the Championship. I rang a friend in Dublin to make an arrangement. His answer unnerved me. "It will be," he said, "like before." I recalled so many 'befores'. "We will take a break," he said, "for a little football on Saturday afternoon." How my mind went back to meeting him and his friends at six of a Friday evening and finding a bed at five on a Saturday morning, and resuming at ten on a Saturday morning and then a match, and then it was Sunday and the plane had been missed, and now it was Monday, and such laughter. But I was younger then. "Look," I said, "I can't face it." At which he in turn said, "Look yourself. Shall I tell you the difference between the Celtic peoples?" "What power on earth," I asked, "could stop you?" "It is this," he said. "The Irish have livers, and the Welsh do not." He may have a point.

Cowardice, therefore, led me to watch the match on television and here were the French once more quarrelling. I recalled a match at Lansdowne Road where even the great Welsh team fell into disarray and lost 14-0 in 1970. The gossip then was that there was some distance between players as great as Gareth Edwards and J. P. R. Williams over some obscure rivalry at Millfield School each had attended. Ireland drew with France with the French scoring tries and Ireland scoring goals. The Irish coach Mick Doyle was reported as saying to his goal-kicker Michael Kiernan that he didn't care if he didn't kick one all season. That is the way to inspire confidence. He kicked five against France. [And went on to win the Championship.]

The game was as rough as any seen in a decade. The referee, Australian Kerry Fitzgerald, talked to *The Guardian*'s Peter Bills afterwards and said:

> The rivalry in Dublin was unhealthy. I wouldn't like to think a game of rugby is played like that every day. Some of the players were going too far. I didn't expect the game to be played with that hidden niggling

attitude and I think it spoiled it. It was a win at all costs situation and the French didn't seem to care how they won. But that's not sport. And rugby ought to be a game played for the enjoyment of everyone.

No one is an angel and the Australians certainly not. If the French this season seemed to be unusually combative I wondered what the reason might be. We are going to France to do some research, perhaps we will find some reason, perhaps to do with competitiveness, or even material reward. In Ireland, where the game is so much that of the professional and often comfortable middle class, one must remember that even the bourgeois Irish can be fiery. Only in Limerick town is the Irish game a working-class one. What was good to see about this Irish team today is that they laughed on the field. I hope they win the Championship if for no other reason than that.

2 March

TGRD   If any position has diminished, not so much in importance as in quality, over the period coaching has established its roots in Welsh rugby, it is that of centre three-quarter. Its role has changed significantly so that general footballing ability and vision have been sacrificed for a more determined physicality. Since the late 'sixties there has been a steady decline in what could be thought of as the traditional role of the position within the team. To begin with, the dispensation law forbidding kicking directly into touch outside the 22-metre line placed emphasis on quick transference of the ball to those wide spaces occupied by the wings and full-back. This relied on good passing in mid-field, in the style of the exemplary John Dawes, and made for attractive and spectacular rugby. It was successful and made sense. Circumstances encouraged inventive and innovative thinking. Then coaching took a firmer grip on matters. 'Gain line', 'good ball' and 'bad ball' began to have a persuasive influence on the way we thought about the game. Most pernicious was 'second phase possession'. This fashioned a whole philosophy. 'Second phase' became an end in itself. Players kicked in order to set it up, forwards charged into the opposition to do so. Players no longer looked to evade the opposition but made a point of knocking into them. Centre three-quarters, so the modern thinking had it, should be chosen for such unenticing forays down the middle.

In this Welsh rugby was largely influenced by New Zealand which had for many years adopted a block-busting charge as part of its tactics. But our coaches, unlike their New Zealand counterparts, became obsessed with this style so that, regardless of the quality of the players at their disposal, a number of straightforward moves were arranged to bring the ball back or near to the forwards, with the centre programmed to charge at players in the middle of the field. It was as subtle and creative as a picket line confrontation and equally damaging to reputations.

Once on this particular treadmill it was difficult to get off. The received wisdom stated that three-quarters could only be effective with a big centre in the middle. The tactics were thought of first and the players had to fit in with the plan. The result was a downward spiral. Running and passing skills were made redundant by such a philosophy. There was no need to perfect them, since they were of limited use in this limited scheme. It must be admitted that, latterly, the laws governing the maul have also assisted in the demise of the skilful passing and running centre.

Fortunately in the past year there seems to have been a recognition of the problem at National level at least and a determination to seek a solution. Players such as David Richards and Bleddyn Bowen, who play at outside-half for their clubs, were chosen at centre for their country. Today against Scotland there were some notable performances from individual players, such as Pickering, Norster and, in difficult circumstances, Holmes. But it was Mark Ring who stood out as a beacon of glittering talent, continuing the trend begun by Bleddyn Bowen in 1983/84 which might hint at the resurgence of the centre three-quarter as an attacking force in his own right in Welsh rugby once more.

Like Terry Holmes, Ring is a Cardiffian with the unmistakable twang of the city, and they both attended Roman Catholic schools, Holmes Bishop Hannan, Ring Lady Mary's High School, which has provided a great tradition of rugby within the city. Like Bowen and Richards before him, Ring has played a lot of his rugby at outside-half. He uses delicate skills rather than unsubtle force, evasion rather than confrontation, the rapier rather than the bludgeon.

Mark Ring, it is said, is not consistent. Mark Ring, if you listen to the critics, makes mistakes. Mark Ring takes time off during the game. He misses tackles, too. Or so say those for whom work rate and high-tech efficiency are the be all and end all of their routine rugby respectability.

But Mark Ring is the player who disrupts the ordinariness of a game. There is cheek and mischief there, a certain arrogance which requires people taking him on his own terms. He may well miss a tackle and perhaps let in a try. But he is the man who will create half a dozen more and he has the ability to transform the present Welsh team to a higher level of potential. In a word, Mark Ring has the 'star' quality which has been so sadly lacking in the British game. When all is said and done it is the expectation of star performance which draws us back time and time again to the terraces. Mark Ring is one very good reason to go and see Cardiff play. And, after those side-steps which gave Pickering his first try at Murrayfield, it may be just the kind of thing which will prompt the Arms Park to sing once more.

"The benevolent spirit of a former match returned on a sentimental visit," I wrote after the game, "and hovered for a full eighty minutes over Murrayfield . . . This game was imbued with some of the brilliant shades of the unforgettable match in 1971." And it was like that, too. There was a lot of running, thrust and counter-thrust, a lot of mistakes as well, but why worry about those as long as there are not too many of them? A benevolent spirit spreads its influence over the Welsh team too. But although it was a good start to the season and achieved a win away from home, some surgery is still needed.

An away win this year ought now to mean a Triple Crown, as the other two games are at home. But is that any longer any source of comfort? Wales have lost their last three games at the Arms Park, once so formidable a bastion for any visiting team.

The victory against Scotland was marred afterwards by some harsh speaking by John Bevan, the Welsh coach. He accused the French referee, René Hourquet, of being 'incompetent' and said that he would not entrust him with charge of a game for his boys at school. While John Bevan is entitled to his opinion (and M. Hourquet did leave something to be desired) there is a time and a place for expressing it. This was not the occasion.

[And it rebounded. Later in the week the WRU dissociated itself from Bevan's remarks.]

4–8 March

TGRD   The announcement of the Welsh team to play Ireland was greeted with what I thought to be, in Philip Larkin's words, 'unignorable silence'. The public after the Murrayfield victory seem to be fairly content with the team. But, as for the last two years, this Welsh team will not be consistently successful because the back row lacks balance. The players in the back row of the scrum must complement each other. There is nothing as yet that binds Pickering, Moriarty and Morris together, fine players though they are individually. Unlike Jeff Squire who was happiest operating close to the scrum to carry out the necessary chores there, Pickering has the instincts of the open-side wing forward and plays as such. Richard Moriarty, too, has neither the bulk nor, more importantly, the inclination to be a work-horse of a flanker. He is an adventurer by instinct, a player who prefers the open spaces to operate in. But that leaves the No. 8 on his own to tighten operations round the shadier channels of the scrum and often means that Terry Holmes has to operate as a fourth back-row forward. This role was once an occasional bonus, but now appears a prerequisite to the way the Welsh team play. Inevitably it diminishes Holmes' effectiveness at scrum-half, and it is taking its toll on his frame.

9 March

JM   Gloucester versus Harlequins at Kingsholm in the John Player Cup quarter final. Here the borders of English rugby meet. The hard men of the West against the Fancy Dans of the Metropolis. The crowd was some 10,000. "Every man in the crowd," I was told in the club beforehand, "knows his rugby because every man has played." I was presented with a copy of the club history. I realised that I was at the hard heart of English rugby. As it turned out the match wasn't like that at all. The only dirty play came from the Harlequins. The team that ran the ball, and won comfortably, was Gloucester. [Much the same was to happen later in the semi-final, when Gloucester played the more attractive rugby against Bath, and Bath won because Gloucester missed a vital kick at goal.]

For me, though, the day was an enchantment for reasons that make rugby a delight for its life-long followers. Chalky White was there, who did so much for

Leicester and who is now in charge of English rugby in the South-West. He said that there was in rugby an innocent freemasonry. And so the day proved. Clem Thomas (RCC that was) came into the bar. I hadn't met him for a long time. The first article I ever wrote about the game was about a match in which Clem played, the game in which Wales beat New Zealand 13-8 in 1953. I wrote, borrowing a line from Dylan Thomas, about him and the other heroes of the day, running on to the 'fields of praise'. I described Clem's cross-kick to Ken Jones and how the wing three-quarter in scoring became immortal with a try. On the strength of that article in the *New Statesman* – I was twenty-three at the time – I became a rugby correspondent for *The Observer*. When I gave up the job in 1959, I handed it over to Clem: he has become one of the best of all rugby writers. He is not well today, having suffered a bad attack of hepatitis.

He was fit enough, however, to join me in a waltz down memory lane, or perhaps a side-step, so characteristic of the charm of the game. As the Irish said: there is this interruption in the afternoon for a little football. I recalled that the last time I had been at Kingsholm was in 1951 when I had been in the RAF up the road at Moreton-in-the-Marsh and was to play for Birmingham. The Gloucester scrum-half was Swansea's Vivian (or Mattie) Davies. Some Swansea members of the RAF team I was in were wondering if Gloucester were short: I was not keen, not being good enough. However, I explained to Clem Thomas, this very day I have heard I am to be made a Fellow of my old university at Swansea and that what delights me most is that among all the distinguished academics I am numbered with, Haydn Tanner is to be so honoured at the same ceremony.

Clem at this point managed to intrude a word. He said that he had won his first cap for Wales in a side captained by Haydn Tanner. He had never known a footballer so assured, so in command of the field. Clem then was, I think, only eighteen: Tanner was in his last season. Wishing, as ever, to bring a tale full circle, I said to Clem that what so connected Haydn Tanner, the Fellowship and playing at Gloucester for me was that Mattie Davies's father, Trevor, had been my woodwork teacher at school. He had thought, when I was very young, that I was a promising player. Therefore he had got me the job of running the touchline at St. Helen's when those fabulous unofficial International matches were played during the second world war in which union and league players ran on together. There was Tanner and Davies, Bleddyn Williams and Gus Risman, those formidable wings like Williams and Alun Edwards: such rugby. The last time I had spoken to Haydn Tanner was as a four-teen-year-old, handing him the ball for a line-out. My diary for 1944 records that I asked him for his autograph, but I think I was speechless. The juvenile diary records a pride in being there. There followed the 'little interruption' in the afternoon which saw Gloucester through to the semi-final, the large crowd affable in the confidence of victory, applauding the Harlequins who were not in the best of spirits, perhaps living in the memory of Gloucester past, puzzled at the new Kingsholm style.

Conversation resumed with Chalky White who offered an incisive analysis of the dilemmas of English rugby. In his view, as I understand it, it is necessary for the best players to stretch themselves. Excellence is important. Fun is also vital, but the means must be found through the structure of league tables to ensure that players confront the best so as to become the best. Affable and haphazard fixtures do not encourage players to sharpen up. The tradition of social enjoyment in the English game comes to militate against reaching the standards that the best of International rugby needs. We talked about the Berry Hill club which I had been following, which he much admired. We went on to consider what would happen were small clubs to enjoy fixtures further afield than those they had known. There was a problem about travelling costs in a game where gate money was small and the price of away games grew. Nevertheless, he believed that players would benefit from standards being raised, which I am sure is the case: pleasure increases in step with talent.

At which I had the pleasure of having my hand read by the mother of the Harlequins and England full-back Marcus Rose. Mrs. Rose had offered the thought that if her legs had been longer her son's might have been, which might have influenced his game. He seemed to me to be playing well enough. I was told – this is the kind of thing you learn at rugby matches – that one's right hand is what one is given; the left is what you make of yourself. Mrs. Rose, an elegant and handsome woman with a voice low and gentle, appropriate to a hand-reader with a nervous customer, was very encouraging. She traced various crises in my life with an accuracy that had me enchanted. Had I, she asked, had a recent trauma? I sure had, I said. Would you believe it, she asked, if I were to say that your life line is stronger since? I would be happy to do so, I said. What would you have done, I asked, if my hand was bad news? I would, she replied, have asked you to buy me an orange juice. Someone, observing the magical display, asked if she would read his hand. Mrs. Rose looked at it and asked him to buy her an orange juice.

16 March

TGRD "Don't you know, it's a wonderful feeling," said the man with the strong Irish brogue at the end of the game, "to be able to leave the Arms Park, smiling." The face of the Irish coach was also beaming afterwards, as he reflected that this was the first time he had wished a Wales v. Ireland match at Cardiff could have gone on for another quarter of an hour. Such was the confidence. He knew, as everybody in the ground knew, that as the second half wore on and errors accumulated, the situation was getting increasingly embarrassing for the Welsh.

Ireland won by the unarguable margin of 21-9. This match more than any other in recent years exemplifies the stagnancy which has settled over the game in Wales. This is a failure to understand the nature of the game, and a misunderstanding of the role of those on the sidelines who control the way the game is played on the field.

If the strategy is determined off the playing field, tactics are what you employ on the field. During the course of any one game there are checks and balances; the game ebbs and flows. The strengths of one side must be pitted against the strengths of the other; each must find and expose the weakness of the other. The good team will employ the tactics best suited to winning the game on the day.

On the evidence of this game and those against France and Scotland at the Arms Park last season, Wales are not doing this.

In concentrating on attacking rugby in Wales, the coaches, selectors and players ignore the tactics by which the game is won. In the end, to run with the ball may be the philosophy or strategy, but within any one game it is only one tactic out of many. As the game evolves over eighty minutes, so also must the players evolve or change the tactics which determine the superiority of one team over the other. Against Ireland, Wales ought to have taken control forward at a point in the second half when the pack seemed to be in the driving seat.

Wales have now lost the last four games at home. England is the only team left not to have won at Cardiff in recent years.

JM This proved to be the most touching and sentimental day I have known for a long, long time.
Morriston, the suburb of Swansea in which I spent most
of my youth, were playing Tumble, a team from the
anthracite coalfield further to the west, beyond Llanelli.
For Tumble it was an important match since, if they could
score a try or two against Morriston, then they would be
guaranteed the West Wales Division A League Championship and thus would become the best team in a hard
school. They were coached by Clive and Alan John,
brothers of Barry. Clive was at the match. For Morriston
it was a less serious matter since, after a brief spell in the
senior division, they were about to be relegated. Later in
the day the celebrated Morriston Orpheus Choir (*Cor
Meibion Treforus*) were giving their fiftieth anniversary
concert in the Tabernacle Chapel, the cathedral of that
most democratic of Welsh nonconformist sects, the Con-
gregationalist or *Annibynwyr*. It was a big day and, for
me, moving since I had both played for the Morriston
club and sung in the choir. The connection between both
remains as close as ever.

What a transformation, though, in the prosperity of
the rugby club. When I had played as a schoolboy
between 1945 and 1947 we would meet at the Prince Inn
and change either at the Graig Infants School or in the
Tabernacle vestry, and climb the hill to the Lan where the
field had a slope of one in four. After the match we would
wash in two five-foot zinc galvanised baths, the water
warmed, I now gather, by a committee man who never
saw the team play. I also now learn that there was a
regulation of the Welsh Rugby Union and the education
authorities that schoolboys were not allowed to play for
the school in the morning and the local club in the
afternoon. If that rule was known, I never remember it
mentioned. Certainly it was never followed. I dare say

nowadays the observance is more honoured than the breach.

My memories of playing for Morriston have become confused in time with those of playing for the Swansea Grammar School, which is not surprising since we had fixtures in the same towns and villages. One distinction between the two teams has a sociological importance which I gather is still relevant. Playing for the Grammar School against Ystylefera, say, or Ammanford, we could expect a rough ride because we were the Swansea Jacks, the big town slickers. At the age of fifteen I was carted off to the Amman Valley hospital with concussion because I'd been kicked in the head for coming from Swansea, only to find my attacker joining me before the end of the game, despatched thither by my friend who was the open-side wing forward. What a way to behave! Matches between our school and Gowerton School were even cancelled because of rough play. At least that was our view: theirs is that we were not worth a fixture. In turn, when we played Cardiff High School, we would treat them as city slickers. Another distinction is that the school would often win matches: Morriston seldom did.

The main reason for this is that the team was not much good but contained within that generalisation – and here fellow-players of the time may have a different recollection – there were certain habits not conducive to success. The fifteen was usually composed of young men, often schoolboys, behind the scrum and of older men, steel and tin workers and coalminers, among the forwards. Often they would come off shift to play. In that time Morriston was a centre of heavy industry, the Swansea Valley in which it lay loud and smoking with furnaces at the Upper Forest and Worcester and Dyffryn, and with many small collieries. The steel workers and colliers considered two or three pints of beer at the Prince proper preparation for a game of rugby.

Often we would play the first half of a match down the

slope, when our forwards would be in fighting form, full of beer, steam and fire. The backs, myself at full-back then, would have a fine time. The second half the pack would be exhausted and our opponents would rush at us young backs and trample all over us and the game, yet again, would be lost; and those of us of a philosophic nature would reflect that there was one of life's lessons to be learned here if only we could put our finger on it.

Therefore, when I drove along Chemical Road to meet David Jones, the club secretary, at a ground new to me, the buds of the past were already in flower. I arrived at a large club house as the Tumble team bus drew up. There were proper dressing rooms. There were three playing fields. How different, I said to David Jones, from the days when we played among the cowpats on the hillside. Here was flat ground on the bed of the valley. He pointed out that, in fact, there had been an unfortunate accident. One of the playing pitches was not in use that day since subsidence from an old colliery had created a hole in the ground. Just as well no one was playing at the time, we agreed.

The Morriston club house is perhaps unusual in that a large window overlooks the first team pitch. The window is in the bar. The bar is by some local regulation allowed to be open during the hour and a half the match is played. This enables spectators to keep out of the weather if, as this day, the rain is heavy. Before the match began we had time to consider the unusual history of the club which gives it a rare distinction in Wales: its fortunes match industrial change.

In the season 1893/94 Morriston played Cardiff, Llanelli, Swansea, Neath, Aberavon, London Welsh, Treorky (*sic*) and took a winter tour to Devonport Albion and Torquay Athletic. It was one of the best of first-class clubs, winning most of its matches. This was because it was one of the main industrial centres in Britain, its coal, copper and other metallurgical industries being made more productive by imported German processes. After the first world war a decline began, matched in the fortunes of the club, and local boys went to play for Swansea instead: there were five Morriston men in the Swansea side which beat the New Zealand All Blacks in 1935. The nadir was reached in the years in which I played. But recovery was soon to come.

The revival was pioneered by a handful of enthusiasts like Robert Gwynne and Leighton Davies. A Treasurer was appointed to rescue the accounting from the backs of envelopes, and an interest-free loan of £750 from the WRU purchased the new ground, on which the match with Tumble had just begun. The pattern was clear: Morriston were spoiling around the scrum, Tumble were trying to move the ball among faster backs. The Morriston tactics, as we watched through the huge bar window, looked effective. I gathered, as we chatted, that the club's turnover every year was £100,000, mostly through the bar. £1,400 was spent annually on players' insurance. A set of jerseys costs £300. The club officials compared their experience with a club like Swansea Uplands on the more salubrious side of town. Morriston was a working-class club; the Uplands middle-class. Lately the latter had held a champagne party and raised £2,000, just like that. Here on the east side it was not so easy. Laundry was more than a £100 a month, did I know?

Paying a little more attention to the play, we saw Tumble score two penalty goals and then after half time score two more. They could not, though, for all their side-stepping, barging, variation of tactics, escape the tackling of the Morriston back row and centre three-quarters. That try they so much wanted to score could not be scored, and as their committee men came from the field into the bar, they were anxious to know how their rivals for the Championship, Ystradgynlais, had done. We didn't know, but one of the Morriston men offered to try and find out. He made a phone call and brought the bad news: Ystradgynlais had scored two tries. Therefore in their next match Tumble really had to score a few. [They were to, and won the title.]

Before the players came into the club house for their sausage and chips, a subject was raised, almost in passing, which delighted me, although it should not have surprised me. Morriston Rugby Club have a choir good enough to join that London Welsh extravaganza at the Royal Albert Hall of one thousand Welsh voices. They would be singing there once more in 1986. And did I know that the Chairman of the Orpheus Choir the previous year had been a former Morriston player, Geoffrey Richards?

As the players arrived a dramatic and encouraging event occurred. The club steward announced that he had just heard that Cardiff had beaten Pontypool 24-3 in the semi-final of the Welsh Cup. Everyone cheered. This acclamation demands analysis. Normally in any part of West Wales any triumph by Cardiff is bad news. Nobody west of Bridgend cares for Cardiff. Therefore when a Cardiff victory is applauded in a Morriston club house, the significance transcends parochialism in a manner difficult for the stranger to comprehend. Here were anti-Cardiff citizens, football players, hard men some of them, some dancers, joined in a judgement about the nature of rugby football. They disliked Pontypool rugby *so* much that they would prefer Cardiff to win. Their instinctive delight at Pontypool's defeat was therefore an aesthetic statement about the nature of the game they played. They were the artists as critic.

Barry John earlier in the season had said that he regarded the morose, remorseless play of the Pontypool side as a 'cancer' in Welsh rugby. His brother Clive, the Tumble coach, who was with us, concurred. There is, as ever, an irony here, since in popular understanding West Wales rugby is as rough as it comes: that understanding is incomplete. Within the toughness of West Wales, whether in Seven Sisters, Tumble, Morriston, Kidwelly, Cefneithin, Llandovery, Gowerton, or wherever, there is an instinctive understanding of the balance of the game. Whatever may be necessary among the forwards must not inhibit the skill of half-back or three-quarter. If there has to be darkness, then equally there has to be light; a harmony that is a part of nature, as we all know, and therefore part of rugby. In this analysis, Pontypool is all darkness; and that cannot be right: and how can it be fun?

We resumed our conversation about the rugby club choir. A remarkable parallel emerged between the problems of men playing rugby for Wales and those singing in the Orpheus Choir whose concert I was about to go and hear. The choir like the Welsh team is amateur; the men are in work and have families. But between now and September they are singing in London, in Brittany, at Chartres, making a television programme, going to Poole, then Chichester and Birmingham. Their rehearsals are as demanding as squad training. It takes a great deal of time and work. And so good singers sometimes opt out of the Orpheus and prefer to sing with the rugby club choir. Among the rugby club choir seventy per cent were Welsh-speaking, as in my childhood in Morriston: among the rugby players only twenty per cent.

I discovered that the present Chairman of the Orpheus Choir was Huw Madoc-Jones, a fellow-member of the RAF Officers Training Corps course at Spitalgate in Lincolnshire early in 1950. If you can manage to live long enough the circles of experience do grow small. I was thus enabled to offer the curious tale of how I came to play rugby with International players. Being no good at firing rifles or Bren guns or flying aeroplanes I realised that the only way I could win a commission was by serious thought. My first step was to seize the editorship of the course magazine and write a flattering portrait – indeed deserved – of the course commander. Within the rugby team there was a severe dispute between two Scottish Internationals and three Welsh players as to who should captain the team. I was proposed as a compromise. Since we played teams who had no players of a comparable standard, we always won. As captain I was given the credit: I also kicked the goals. I did little else at outside-half but give the Dalgleishes the ball. Therefore, I recounted, I became an officer in the RAF. Later this evening Hugh Madoc-Jones thought my account may have some truth in it.

At which some of us set off for Tabernacle with its grand spire and Welsh baroque interior. When young I used to find it not at all confusing that on a Saturday afternoon we would change in the vestry to go and play up the hill and then spend the evening in the chapel with the Orpheus Choir listening perhaps to Kathleen Ferrier and Heddle Nash sing like angels.

I was wearing now the Morriston Rugby Club tie with which I had been presented. It bears the emblems of the town's Castle Graig and St. John's Church which, in the days I went there with my mother, conducted its services in Welsh. It was now that the day truly became awash in sentiment in a style that may be foreign to rugby clubs elsewhere but is not peculiar in Wales.

When the concert began and I saw in the Orpheus Choir members of the rugby club, that direct and untroubled connection in a Welsh society acquired a strength that was memorable. My mother had been a friend of the first conductor of the Morriston Orpheus, Ivor Sims, who had made it in the 'forties one of the world's great choirs. I dare say that was one reason why I was permitted to be a second tenor in its still-celebrated recording of 'Y Delyn Aur' and 'Myfanwy'. That was in 1947. The choir had sung at my grandfather's funeral.

The soloists this evening were Dennis O'Neill, who came back for the occasion from the Metropolitan Opera in New York and another local star, Eiddwyn Harry. Both, as did the choir, sang their hearts out. We applauded until we almost broke our wrists and were not at all embarrassed by our tears. I doubt if there were many in the audience unmoved by the knowledge that a choir begun by Ivor Sims half a century before should be still so eloquent in its harmonies and sophisticated in its techniques. That the rugby club should have been so transformed in the meantime may not have been on their minds that dazzling evening: it was on mine.

23–31 March

TGRD The International Board have agreed to inaugurate a World Cup or, in their words, an International Tournament, in 1987. This is a bold step for a group not noted for its boldness. It was only a few months ago I met Sir Nicholas Shehadie of Australia and Dick Littlejohn of New Zealand in the North British Hotel in Edinburgh when they were over to see the SRU in the last of their meetings with the four Home Unions. Both of them had prepared a paper and had assessed the possibilities for such a competition. They must have been remarkably persuasive to prompt an essentially conservative committee to immediate action. It has been positively impulsive compared with their usual procrastination. There are no sub-committees, no delaying referrals, simply a statement of fact. There will be an International Tournament held in Australasia in 1987. For once the International Board would seem to have had their ears to the ground to good effect, for generally speaking the players are in favour of such a competition, provided, of course, they rationalise the rest of the International programme of tours and matches accordingly.

Going to Hong Kong and seeing the Sevens competition there gives a taste in miniature of what might be possible. Here in a colony with no tradition of rugby, apart from what the expatriates have imported, is a lively competition full of colour and festival mood. Here are Thailand, Singapore, the Solomon Islands and Samoa harmonising after their fashion with New Zealand and Australia. The Irish Wolfhounds, Crawshay's, the Public Schools Wanderers and the French Barbarians are here, if unavoidably weakened by rearranged International fixtures in Europe. It is a worthy and successful competition, from which the International Board can learn something in their preparation for the World Cup.

Here the race will be to the strongest and the swiftest. The World Cup will be about that too. But not, one hopes, to the exclusion of all else. Inevitably in the first competition there will be the division between the International Board nations and the rest. But it is important that those knocked out in the early stages should be able to retain their interest and have a part to play to the end of the competition. A Plate or Bowl, run in tandem with the Cup proper, might be the answer.

The Australians are hissed like pantomime villains when they come on the field. It reminds me of the way London Welsh are traditionally greeted at Twickenham in Middlesex Sevens. So I know Australia won't be minding at all. When you're the top dog you can enjoy the discomfited yowls of the opposition. We were all happy, however, to hail the Wallabies as conquering heroes when they won the competition.

They could well have won the cabaret at the official dinner afterwards as well. This cabaret is an integral part of the weekend and each team has to provide suitable entertainment. The Australians were finely upstaged by the Samoan manager who sang a romantic ballad in the best Las Vegas tradition and brought the house down. I wonder whether a similar party spirit will prevail in Auckland for the World Cup final in the summer of '87?

JM How glum the Welsh team look in the departure lounge at Cardiff airport as we set off for Paris. They do not look like young men out for a game in France. There is no laughter. Rhys Williams, the former Llanelli and Wales forward, one of the selectors, is cheerful enough considering the opprobrium the Big Five have attracted to themselves this season. In 1969, when I was involved in uproar about the South African rugby tour to Britain, Rhys had exhibited a characteristic piece of Welsh charm in the Cardiff club. He was disputing my attitude to South Africa with me when our conversation was interrupted by a South African abusing me. Rhys told him to mind his own business. It was all right for him to criticise me: it was not for the South African to do so.

The arrangements at our various hotels in Paris are not ideal. At mine I found a man asleep in the room I had been given. Two colleagues had been put in attic elsewhere, objected, and were moved to an hotel where there were no rooms at all. When we met to brood on these difficulties I tried to cheer up the company by recounting how once at the Chelsea Hotel in New York I had been given a room where there was a corpse in the bed; not that the management could be held completely to blame for that sad denouement. We decided to eat at a favourite restaurant, Le Muniche, across the river in the Rue de Seine, a district where I mostly stay on account of the market and the cheapness of the hotels.

We were, as often one is, puzzled as to why we had come to Paris at least a day earlier than we need have done to see Wales play. I suspect the spare day is to reminisce about previous excursions before clearing the mind's palate to imprint the future memory. I recalled a year when a celebrated performance of *Don Giovanni* at the Opera House with a mainly Welsh cast had coincided with the game. Margaret Price, Sir Geraint Evans, Stuart

Burrows and Robert Lloyd had been on stage. The performance was memorable not only for the quality of the singing but for the awesome set which moved towards the audience from time to time filling all with fear that it would sweep the distinguished performers into the orchestra and collapse on all of us.

I wrote an *Observer* atmosphere piece about that particular year's Welsh invasion of Paris in terms of *Don Giovanni*. But it was a tragedy, for Wales were expected to lose. It was on the same trip that I achieved what I still boast of as a fine coup. My friend Siân Lloyd was in Paris. She wanted to see the game. No tickets were to be found. I had a press ticket. My plan therefore became clear. I would introduce her into the Press Box. This idea, arrived at late in the evening, was treated derisively by the shrewd company she and I were keeping. Bets were laid that it was an impossible dream. No woman had ever been seen in the Press Box at the Parc des Princes to anyone's knowledge; and without a pass it was incomprehensible that anyone could reach the privileged place.

At the outer gate of the stadium half an hour before the kick-off we met the police. I explained to them that while it was certainly the case that I had only one press ticket and that the young woman was without one, this was due to an oversight. She was, in fact, my interpreter. It was necessary for me to write about the match in both English and Welsh but my Welsh was inadequate. Therefore she needed to translate my piece. The argument was not impressing them. Suddenly, as these ideas do come from time to time, I wondered if either of the policemen was a Breton. One was. A conversation was opened on the similarities between the Breton and Welsh languages. We were through the outer gate. The wind was now with us. Because we had been allowed to approach the Press Box the authorities there presumed it must be all right or we wouldn't be there. A further flurry of chat

119

in French and Welsh and there we were among the cognoscenti of the game in Britain and Europe. Surprise was soon followed by the paying off of bets. My friend not being normally a rugby fan was perhaps not sensitive either to the scale of the achievement, but that didn't matter. Mischief is its own reward at the worst of times; when accompanied by courtesy to women how much more it satisfies. Wales lost that match.

29 March

JM   The French press does not read too well about our prospects for the game. There is still bad feeling about John Bevan criticising the French referee after our match at Murrayfield. Hints like fists forecast trouble. We solemnly agreed, in the splendour of the foyer of the Hotel Concorde St. Lazare where we have come to rest, that John Bevan should have given more thought to the welfare of his players when they step out on to the Parc des Princes tomorrow, and then turned our minds to other matters. The Concorde has a mirror in the foyer ceiling, reflecting its baroque and terraced glories. If you are at all unstable it is easy to fall over backwards contemplating the unusual view.

Phil Bennett and Ray Gravell arrive, Ray without his beard, looking younger and more gentle than his ferocious repute on the field might ever suggest. We talk about the native language in Welsh rugby and especially in Llanelli. I remind them that in 1955 fourteen of the Llanelli team spoke Welsh. How many now do? Three it seems, or four if Ray is playing. This does not necessarily mean that the language has suffered so sharp a decline in the Llanelli hinterland as perhaps that more players come to Stradey nowadays from English-speaking districts to the east and west.

We then talked about that wonderful day when Llanelli beat the All Blacks in 1972. I had spent the week before the game with Carwyn James and the team making a film for Harlech TV. Phil Bennett now revealed some detail which had escaped me certainly at the time of that damp, misty triumph, a game as intense in its passion as any I have seen or anyone involved has ever played in. A critical moment in the victory, said Phil Bennett, had been at a dinner in the club house the Saturday before the Tuesday's match. The team had been cast down to hear of the huge New Zealand victory over Western Counties. Carwyn James had been to see that game. He returned to Stradey, stood at the dinner and announced to his team that he was completely confident that Llanelli would beat the All Blacks. His astonished fifteen at once trusted him.

Phil Bennett believes the match was won in the first two minutes. The Llanelli team had been fired in the dressing room both by Carwyn's careful instructions and by Delme Thomas' moving, patriotic address. Carwyn had also arranged another subtle move. When the teams were on the field it was announced over the loudspeakers that the New Zealand national anthem would be played, at which 'God Save the Queen' rang out. The crowd burst into laughter to the mystification of the All Blacks. The key moment, the decisive stroke, in Phil Bennett's view, came when the Llanelli forwards carried out Carwyn's ploy of hitting the All Blacks' formidable forward Kirkpatrick very hard as soon as he received the ball. In my recollection four Llanelli forwards arrived on him together. Phil Bennett says that he looked into the eyes of the All Blacks at that moment and realised that they were beaten. The powerful force of the psychological element in a big game is not always easy to appreciate from the touchline. There can seldom have been a better, more memorable example.

Phil went on to describe the next match Llanelli played after this famous victory – at Richmond. In the intervening three days most of the Llanelli team and indeed most male citizens of the district had been drunk most of the time. The evening and night of the match I had been staying at the Cawdor Hotel at Llandeilo nearby. Although I was the only resident in the bar it was crowded into the small hours. We were waiting for Carwyn to arrive. The barman said he wished to close; a senior policeman present delicately suggested that the licence might not be secure if the bar closed before the great man arrived. It stayed open.

By Saturday the Llanelli team were in poor shape. Carwyn James insisted that most of them play at Richmond. Phil Bennett reports that going on the field he could see forty-five Richmond players; his comrades scarcely knew which of the three-for-every-one they should tackle. Within two minutes the outside-half was required to kick at goal and for the only time in his career hit the corner flag. The defeat was the heaviest Llanelli had ever suffered at Richmond. When Phil Bennett left the field Carwyn put his hand on his shoulder and said: "Well played, Phil!"

The day was long. I had hoped to steal some secrets from Ieuan Evans who is chairman of the committee reporting on the state of Welsh rugby, but he refused to offer any. Instead we talked of his father's Marxist days in Ammanford, of the anarchists there, of Aneurin Bevan and Jim Griffiths, Arthur Horner and Will Paynter and other heroes of the South Wales miners we had known and of Welsh teams of the past. Men from Ystradgynlais wondered what their chances were of winning the West Wales Championship over Tumble. A group from Bridgend and Aberavon discovering that I was writing a book with Gerald asked if, for a small sum, I would mention their names. Singing broke out, as it will, and early in the morning a group from the Swansea Valley arrived in the hotel having taken three hours to walk the one mile from the Pigalle. They thought they may have lost their way. A party from Aberavon, not feeling too well, were looking for the doctor who had come with them. They discovered he was ill in bed.

30 March

JM   Began the day with a long walk through the Louvre hoping to find the Holbein exhibition of which I'd read. By arriving at the wrong entrance I took in old familiars of Egyptian antiquity, the Winged Victory, Italian Renaissance paintings and, flagging, in the end had time only to consider the Master's portrait of Erasmus, a representation so alive as to lead you to suppose you were in the presence of the thinker. On this high note I set off to meet friends for lunch, observing that there were several at the Louvre wearing Welsh Rugby Union blazers. What a cultivated lot we are an English friend said.

Over lunch at the Brasserie Lipp an important decision was taken. Since friends were going to the match, I would watch it in a mixed company of French and Welsh people who had no tickets, preferably on a large television screen, if one could be found. Gossip flowed. The HTV film crew were having trouble in being given permission to enter the Parc des Princes, the authorities retaliating at what was held to be a lack of co-operation by the Welsh Rugby Union with a French crew at the Wales and Ireland match. There were rumours of a threat to assassinate the South African referee, Mr. Strydom. The French Rugby Federation was thought to be anxious to play an International match at Toulouse rather than Paris, since they believed the people in charge of the Parc des Princes had not made enough effort to have the ground unfrozen for the Welsh match to have been played in January.

This last was an argument appreciated by some Welsh supporters who had told us on the flight from Cardiff that they had gone to Paris in the cold and had a miserable time, and had now to pay yet again to see their heroes play. Those this time without tickets did not seem too depressed: the trip also is important. It reminded me of the time in the 'fifties when Twickenham matches were made all-ticket and of men who had risen with the dawn and travelled on the excursion train to London and had listened to the match on the radio in a pub near the ground.

I arrived at the hotel to watch the game on a huge screen and in the course of the evening was to see it twice more on the same screen among crowds that grew larger and, unfortunately, more critical of the Welsh performance. There were many who had been at the ground and felt that, contrary to all form and all expectation, Wales had played well enough perhaps to have won. Why, oh, why, the argument began, did Moriarty give away that penalty in the first minutes in the Welsh 22? Why did Gareth Davies wait until the second ruck before trying his drop at goal? Had he tried at first, surely he would have scored. Why did wing three-quarter Hadley not turn inside Blanco to score under the posts rather than try and beat him on the outside and so find himself tackled at the corner flag? Why, when centre three-quarter Ring made his brilliant break, one of a quality which should always ensure a try in an International match, were there only two front-row forwards in support? Where was the back row, the half-backs, a wing three-quarter? Instead of a draw or a win Wales lost 14-3 – the biggest margin ever against France.

Admiration was expressed for the new young full-back, Thorburn of Neath, for Mark Ring and for the Welsh front and second rows; sympathy for Terry Holmes, the Welsh captain, at not being guarded by his forwards properly. But mainly the talk was praise of the French full-back, Serge Blanco. Seeing the first French try so often on the screen heightened admiration for Blanco. He had been decisive in entering the three-quarter line when the attack, or *charge*, as the French commentators have it, was towards the right corner flag. He then ran over the touchline and was off the field as the movement continued to the left. He returned, running at great speed flat across the field to take a quick, flip, reverse pass from his outside-half, and was able to move through a gap which made it easy for the left wing three-quarter, Esteve, to score. This was play of the highest quality, as indeed was his intervention in the movement leading to the second French try late in the match. Although the French did not win the Championship, having drawn at Twickenham and Lansdowne Road, the panache of these movements suggested that it should have been theirs.

The Welsh team gathered in their hotel in black ties, once more a despondent group to observe on their way to the mirrored splendour of the dining room at the Grand Hotel. Some Frenchmen told me that these dinners at which the two teams and officials meet are nothing like as friendly as once they were; that the party is soon over, the old camaraderie gone; all now too solemn; bickering between Unions too well remembered.

The evening and night flickered. I met my old friend at La Coupole where some Welsh supporters were singing quietly. The hotel was crowded when we returned, many complaining about the price of beer at £2.50 a pint, others indifferent to cost or, it seemed, anything at all. I tried, duty bound, to interrogate two former Internationals to gauge their view of the match's quality but with no luck. It took me a few minutes to realise that they had been deprived of the power of speech through the day's exertions. Their lips moved but no sound emerged. This matchless image seemed to me to sum up so much that I went to bed while it was fresh in my mind's eye.

JM   Someone found a bottle of champagne for breakfast. It struck me that more champagne had been 'found' on this trip than I remembered in the past. This may be a case, to coin a phrase, of cultural reversion, the French custom, having spread to Britain, now being returned. We calculated how much it was safe to drink since later that evening some of us would have to drive home from airports in Britain.

The Welsh team have already flown home. Why did they have to get up at the crack of dawn to catch a plane back to Cardiff? Why couldn't they have had a little longer in bed, or taken, as we proposed to do, an early lunch and a stroll in Paris with wives or girl friends? For that matter, if a player had wanted to stay on until Monday, why couldn't he have been allowed to do that too? There is certainly enough money coming into the WRU to pay for this simple reward of some leisure in an attractive foreign city. Surely defeat can't have become a disaster of such magnitude on the Richter Scale that they can only think of slinking home in disgrace?

Myself, I had managed to be removed from the team's flight to a later one. One happy consequence of this was to meet a small group at Orly airport who offered an unexpected insight into how the truly prosperous can behave. A Cardiff factory owner, after telling me he had just bought a Jacobean mansion in South Wales, showed me his bill from the Concorde St. Lazare. The cost of drinks from the bar in his room over the three days was £1,600. It must, I said, have been like Paddington Station. It was, he said. My bill was £8.00.

At Cardiff airport, in a cloudburst, I offered my long-term parking ticket to the man at the gate and asked how much I owed. "You've been here too long to pay," he said. What can that mean?

9

April

Now in reality, the world have paid too great a compliment to critics, and have imagined them men of much greater profundity than they really are.

Henry Fielding

Easter Weekend

TGRD   The news that the Barbarians are to discontinue their traditional Easter tour opening fixture with Penarth from next year gives pause for reflection. They've already dropped the Newport game. The trend is not encouraging. Their fiercest followers would have to admit Penarth do not provide even adequate opposition these days. But the club is delighted to entertain their illustrious visitors, hoping that sooner or later their fortunes may change. It is the highlight of their season and brings in much needed income too. For the Baa-Baas it is a good fixture to start the tour. Why should they arrange a tougher one, with Cardiff and Swansea to come?

It is yet another symptom of the times. We need a change of attitude in Welsh rugby. We need to establish the correct number of games per season which will balance a good competitive, combative element against the vitality of the fun factor. The Barbarians are fun.

12 April

JM   In the end this HTV filming trip to the South of France was to be an entertainment: in the beginning it promised to be a fiasco. When Gerald and I arrived hungry at Rodez in pouring rain with the temperature at 32°F, we learned that our luggage had been lost in Paris.

Don Llewellyn, our director, and John Welch, the former
Llanelli player who lives in this small steel town and who
is to be our guide, came to the airport with more bad
news. Because of a bomb scare at Heathrow yesterday,
the film crew had missed the flight from Paris to Rodez
and had had to fly to Toulouse, from where they had had
a long drive. The glamour of television reporting is not
always quite as the world supposes. We, Gerald and I,
had left Newport railway station at eleven a.m.: it was
now ten p.m.

However, spirits were raised when we reached the
hotel. Here was a restored twelfth-century château, the
Hôtellerie de Fontagnes. The dining room is large with
an ancient ceiling, our table round and big enough for the
eight of us. Oysters and wine lift the weary heart. John
Welch offers a long and thorough analysis of the character of local rugby and promises us a journey tomorrow to
a farm-restaurant where, during the Vichy regime, rugby
players travelled to eat well and illegally. We would
discover for ourselves that this part of France, the
Aveyron, would very strikingly resemble West Wales
both in its appearance and industrial and social
character.

13 April

JM The tone of the day was set early when it became
clear that an old game of 'conversation-stopping' was
part of the company's mood. We had a two-hour drive
ahead to the frontier of the Aveyron and Cantal, towards
the river Lot and the Massif Central. John Welch was to
drive us in a hired car since he had smashed his own
against a telegraph post the week before. This knowledge might in other circumstances have disturbed our
confidence, but mysteriously we were in cheerful mood
at moving into a new and interesting experience. The sun
shone from time to time.

The contours of the countryside are indeed like West Wales. This might have been the Swansea or Towy or Teifi Valleys. Here too are industrial settlements, as it might be Gwaun-Cae-Gurwen or, further west, Drefach Velindre in lovely country on the Teifi. Many of the collieries here had been closed and miners had moved away so that second homes are cheap at £12,000. The steelworks still prosper, though, specialising in refined products.

John Welch explained that good rugby players are always given jobs in the works. The game is an earnest matter, local pride engaged in success. He himself came here from playing for Llanelli to coach a side and has prospered as a journalist and film-maker. At his house, large and antique, he had eight paintings by the Welsh artist John Uzzel Edwards, one of miners, others of formal Welsh groups. John wonders that more players from Britain don't come to France (or indeed go to Italy) where rugby is so well-regarded and well-rewarded a game.

It was Don Llewellyn who had devised the original rules for our game of 'conversation-stopping'. They have to be true remarks, made in all good faith, that silence the company either by the extravagance of their claims or their unexpected context. I had been introduced to the game two years earlier when Don and I were working together in Chicago and I happened to remark: "I once knew an Egyptian princess and we sailed on the Nile in Cairo. Later I took her to a *Private Eye* cricket match." Last night our sound recordist, Meurig Thomas, observed, "There's really only one way to travel in the Falklands I always say. And that's by Chinook helicopter." On the drive today to the village of St. Julien de Pignol I was held to have produced another as we climbed above the river Lot: "I think that's where I almost bought a small château in 1973." The company at first thought this a disqualified remark, since it could not be true. However, it was true.

For the same low price we ended up instead on the Welsh border from where it is comparatively more feasible to make a living.

Conversation returned to the socio-economic resemblances between this part of France and West Wales, and we wondered whether the match we are to see tomorrow will be like one between Morriston and Tumble.

Gerald said: "My father always believed that the Morriston Orpheus used to get given complimentary tickets for the North Enclosure at the Arms Park." And he earned himself a conversation-stopping point.

We reached the farm-restaurant Chez le Maria Tou. The walls of the room were rough. The fireplace was a cavern. Sides of bacon hung over the wood fire. Our long table was old. After a while the local clientele began to shout messages across to us when they realised that we were interested in rugby. All the men seemed to have played long ago.

What kind of meal then did they eat, those players who had come here secretly during the war and openly since? We began with onion soup. Smoked pork was followed by a pork terrine. We moved from a local *grappe* to a wine which seemed to have a suitable name for the occasion, *Buzet*. Chickens arrived with a memorable garlic stuffing. The next dish puzzled us. There was fish certainly, but cooked with a cheese and yellow vegetable hard to place. Local cheeses were then eaten and a prune tart.

It was now that the trouble began and we were offered an insight both into the universal tastes of rugby players and perhaps, also, the peculiar fortitude of the French. The proprietors, both very old, decided that we were friendly invaders and offered us a home-made prune brandy. Having, a few years earlier, been paralysed elsewhere in the Languedoc drinking *framboise*, I should have advised my colleagues against that kind of French drink. However, as the lyricist has it:

The will is strong
The won't is weak.

Therefore we neglected the message that home-made prune brandy has two powerful characteristics: the swiftness and certainty with which it hits the target. Pointing this out to our generous friends, they replied that the only answer to this condition was an unusually curative champagne. It was at this critical moment in the day that the neighbouring tables began singing French rugby airs.

We decided, courteously, to respond. I offered the theory that 'Sospan Fach', that melancholy Llanelli air, is written on a tenth-century atonal scale, even if many people didn't know so. Therefore we would sing it in that style. I tried so to conduct it and lead the singing. Sadly a dispute broke out between the faction which supported me, and a school which preferred to know 'Sospan Fach' as a battle cry. As so often happens in company to do with rugby football, there was fractious patter. "I could murder a pint of Brains SA," said someone. "SA means Skull Attack," said Gerald. "In that case," said our Production Assistant (PA) Sue Hopkins, "PA means Prune Attack."

"I don't think the Welsh as a race are ready for prune brandy," was Don Llewellyn's grave conclusion.

16 April

JM I begin to think that rugby pervades all. I mention to the film director Richard Watkins who will be making some sense of three short films I'm to write for the Welsh-language television channel, that I'd been looking at rugby in the South of France. At which he revealed that he had played for Grenoble. This was in the late 'sixties. He had gone there to improve his French. He went to the rugby club hoping for a game – he had played for a second-class club in his native Swansea. He was selected as the first team scrum-half and so played against all the great French players of the time. Occasionally he played at centre three-quarter against men like Camberabero and Boniface. Richard is a stocky man in his thirties now, not tall, but then he was slim. He was astonished to find that so many of the most celebrated of French backs were no bigger than him.

Richard thinks he is the only player in French rugby who was flown to London to have contact lenses made at a club's expense. This came about after a Cup match which Grenoble won by a dropped goal to nil, to the ultimate pleasure of a crowd of some 15,000 strong. During the course of the match Richard did not give a single pass to his outside-half. The crowd had been a bit puzzled, even cross at this: his backs were furious. But it was the first time they had played in the rain. His eyesight was so bad that, given the weather, he could not even see his fly-half and so kicked or ran with his back row the whole match. With his contact lenses his style was transformed.

Even in those days – and Richard must have been one of the first of British players to enjoy French rugby club life – the club paid for his flat and gave him a generous petrol allowance in cash. It also provided a high class of girl for the bachelor players, or others, after the game. As he says, being eighteen at the time, he learned a lot.

He admits to a bad game in Paris. He was playing in the trial match for selection to play the New Zealand All Blacks, once more in the centre. He knew he did not have any hope but so pleased was he at being selected that he celebrated all the night before. He was in such poor shape on the field that the first pass he received knocked him out and he was taken off injured. He played for one minute. A year later he moved to the United States and became the rugby coach at the rich Californian University of Stanford. He enjoyed that also.

20 April

TGRD   Wales v. England: England remain the only National team not to win at the Arms Park in recent years and must still look back to 1963 for the last taste of victory here. For Wales, this match provided yet another graphic demonstration of the need to find a much tighter unit in the back row. Whilst the front five of the scrum may very well form the cornerstone of a team and the half-backs choose the patterns, the overall structure of that team, and the way it wishes to play, can crumble if the back row does not exert its influence. It is the grouping of these players which can, on the one hand, expose most effectively the limitations of the opposition, whilst, if it lacks substance, it can restrict significantly the ambitions of its own team. The individual members of the Welsh back row have for the past two years failed to complement each other and have been extravagantly inefficient. Davies, Roberts and Pickering now give a semblance, at least, of substance. Each was rubbing shoulders with the other on most occasions. Significantly at that moment when they were all there together for the conclusive final try, theirs was the vital contribution to the victory. With a tighter, more forceful presence in front of him, Holmes, for the first time this season, was able to fulfil himself as a dominating scrum-half, as he does for Cardiff, rather than, as has been foisted upon him by Wales, play out his role as a fourth member of a hitherto inadequate back row.

20 April

JM   To travel from Chepstow to Cardiff for a Wales and England match clarifies the conflict. The train arrived from Gloucester and Lydney. It was crowded when it arrived at the border. The day was clear but cold, fine for football. Before the train from England arrived there had been the usual informed gossip on our platform that an earlier train had been cancelled and that therefore ours would be packed. It was. Not since the war have I seen a set of carriages so crowded. My son had known nothing like it, everyone shoulder to shoulder, chest to chest, white and scarlet together. A few held cans of beer above their heads and poured like fountains. There was no bad feeling at all but, rather, general laughter that so many people should be together on a train.

At a party at the Angel Hotel before the match, where we were filming, I was struck at how the English present stood differently from the Welsh. The generalisation may be unfair, but the visitors stood with their feet apart, as if standing their ground; the Welsh leaned forward more, as if about to pounce. This could well have been because the English expected to be attacked while the Welsh had it in mind to pounce. That day I had been asked to help with a campaign to save Madame Adelina Patti's opera house at Craig-y-Nos in the Swansea Valley from a possible harmful sale. There were several choristers in the company. I appealed to their musical and sporting nature by telling them that the great prima donna Patti had been keen on sport. She supported the Abercrave Rugby Club. More, she used to play snooker in the village and drink pints of beer. Did they know that she was bald? Wore a wig?

At the match we sat, as we had been doing since 1968, in our Debenture seats. I had bought them against my will, believing the principle was wrong. My moral argument was overborne by the Welsh Rugby Union who said they needed the money. At this match we had for the first time a truly tedious neighbour. "Kick," he kept on shouting to the Welsh half-backs. "Make ground." But whatever the team did was wrong when, for the first time for two years, they kept doing things more or less right. Every time he shouted his advice, the team did the converse and scored. This did not stop him shouting the same wrong advice again. I wondered what he was like at home.

JM   In The George at St. Briavels I am told by a friend that the Wales v. England match had been video-recorded for despatch to Holland. Since this may not be a permitted transaction I won't mention his name. He adds that, on the whole, the Dutch are not too interested in Home Championship matches, preferring games in which France or other foreign sides are involved. He adds that there is a lot of traffic of this kind between Britain and the rest of Europe. His account of a game he was present at between Hilversum and Utrecht did not surprise me. The first quarter-hour was undiluted pugilism. I said that it was normal for forwards to test the temper of the opposition in this manner. No, no, he replied: this was different. Fisticuffs are a ritual beginning to a game. He thought this surprising in a people of such high repute as the Dutch. I offered the thought that I had discovered to my surprise in Indonesia that the brutality of the Dutch as a colonial power there had led the locals to hail the Japanese as liberators during the last war. And where, I said, did the Afrikaner come from in South Africa?

My friend had played for Gloucester but the afternoon before had been doing some ratting for a friend with his ferret. I asked him if it was true that rats carried off ducks' eggs by holding them on their stomachs while comrades tugged them away. It was. He then went off to send his video-tape of the match to Amsterdam.

JM   Several enthusiasts missed the Wales and England match yesterday because they were at the wedding at Maesteg between the BBC broadcasting wit Patrick

135

Hannan and Menna, the latter a Bridgend supporter. They all had tickets but, of course, the game had been postponed from February. Two other fans present, also broadcasters, Geraint Talfan Davies and the former Glamorgan cricketer, Peter Walker, hit on a scheme. They would use the hymn board to keep the gathering in the chapel aware of the score. It is impossible to discover whether this devoted plan was actually carried out. One source says the tale is apocalyptic – a good choice of word; most would have said apocryphal. Another says it happened. In Welsh rugby the truth is seldom an improvement on the wish, but when it is, it becomes history; when it isn't, it becomes legend.

26 April

TGRD   This week Clive Rowlands, coach to the Welsh team of the late 'sixties and 'seventies, has decided that he no longer wishes to be on the panel of selectors next season. He wants to take a break from it all and recharge the batteries, he says. At this critical time for the game in Wales it is worth recollecting that it was partly through Clive's efforts that the Welsh team established an identity in the six years between 1968 and 1974. With his sense of fun and camaraderie he melded together a bunch of very talented players into a team with a recognisable spirit. It is worth remembering his ability to manage his men and the way he responded to the public-relations side of the post when, nowadays, such talents are sadly lacking.

It has been a joyless season for Welsh rugby, not because the team could only end up in the middle of what many considered to be the second division table of the Five Nations Championship, but, more disconcertingly, because of the many rumours of discontent which have arisen from the Welsh ranks. We are persuaded to believe that playing rugby is meant to be for enjoyment.

But there has been little evidence emerging from the Welsh squad to suggest that this was so in their case. By all accounts they were not the happy few, nor were they, selectors, coaches and players, a band of brothers. Appearances at squad training were grudging, not only because there were too many of them, but because it was all done with such unsmiling seriousness. Such tight-lipped acceptance was not good for morale, nor were the tales told out of school. An unhappy atmosphere prevailed. The players admitted it.

This has been overwhelmingly confirmed over the past two seasons by the increasing number of players who have called it a day at International level while continuing to appear for their clubs. Graham Price, in the opening chapter of his autobiography, gives a scornful account of the treatment which the players received. He was the first to go, followed by Jeff Squire. Both were in the twilight of their careers but who would deny that had they been available they would still have been in the Welsh team. David Richards, the Swansea centre, took the same path, as did, more surprisingly, in December the then captain of Wales, Mike Watkins, followed by Eddie Butler and at the end of the season Gareth Davies. In these latter instances the players' announcements seem to have been timed to cause maximum embarrassment to the selectors who contrived to make matters worse for themselves by appearing to bungle a few decisions. Selection, after all, is a matter of opinion which, in a group of five, can be adjusted and modified. Or, if there is no consensus it can be put to the vote. Argument there will be as to who is the better of two outside-halves in Wales. That is understandable and the debate, especially in Wales, will not end there of course. But that is in the nature of things.

But in the last year the selectors had committed errors of judgement – over Alun Davies' match fitness, David Waters' omission from the squad and subsequent selection, the incredible dropping of Terry Holmes, and that final straw, the inclusion, despite all the talent available, of that stranger, A.N. Other, at outside-half before the England match. It had come to a pretty pass that, after eight months of rugby in which the International season had been extended by three weeks, the selectors were unable to make up their minds as to who should occupy that princely position which is the nation's pride and joy. Worse, they made the whole matter depend on a weekend's performance. Gareth Davies decided not to take part in a petty and embarrassing scheme. The selectors were immediately seen as the villains whilst Gareth Davies in retirement became a hero.

To the public the WRU's dour and grim approach seemed to be confirmed on radio and television which is the only point of contact the public has with those in charge of a great and much-cherished tradition. The WRU spokesmen were found to be lacking in warmth and vitality. The media can often be seen as intrusive but it will not go away, and sooner or later the WRU and their representatives will have to come to terms with it. They might like to take a leaf out of Alan Jones book, or that of Mick Doyle of Ireland, both of whom seemed to revel in the spotlight.

There is also a lack of communication within the squad itself. For many years it has been the understanding that no player, apart from the captain and any new caps, can be interviewed unless permission has first been sought and granted from the WRU. This was seen as a means of protecting players from undue pressure. In fact some of today's players would prefer not to have such a low profile thrust upon them. Some would simply like to be seen on the telly. Others candidly admit it would enhance their job promotion prospects as a public-relations exercise for their firms. International squad training ought to be a matter not just of coaching and teaching but of man management and organisation. The fact that the squad members are among the elite of players should be enough testimony to their skill. Why else are they there? Managing men is part and parcel, too, of public relations.

These matters need some urgent revision with the World Cup in 1987. In a changing, more sophisticated rugby world the men in charge then will be in a position to enhance or diminish the image of the Welsh game. Now is the time to consider the man chosen to manage the Welsh team, who should be chosen for his ability to manage men. This position is usually filled by an internal appointment from the WRU committee. That a man good enough for the job should emerge by this process will be pure chance. Perhaps the man appointed for this unique role should not necessarily come from within the Welsh Rugby Union? The net should be cast wider than that.

26 April

JM   John Belcher, the Press Secretary of Berry Hill, called this afternoon with more detail of the club's finances after its successful season. He told me, in passing, that the club had beaten the South Glamorgan Institute, a fine Welsh student team, by 16-3. Geraint John, whom many think may be the next Welsh outside-half, played on the wing for the students. It had been a wet and windy night. The students' problem had been that their front five could not, as is bound to happen with young teams, hold the Berry Hill front five. Therefore they needed to run the ball. In the conditions this was a poor compensatory tactic since when the youngsters dropped the ball, the Berry Hill back row ran through and scored.

He had the figure for what the John Player Cup run had been worth to the club that season: £3,000. This was going to be a help with the cost of tarmacadaming the car park which, even with so many club members giving their labour free, would be some £7,000.

He raised a question that, he said, was beginning to engage the club. Should they charge gate money? I hadn't realised they did not. Their approach was to pass a box around. This seemed to them best suited to the game's amateur character and he thought that they would probably go on doing so, while finding small sponsors to help expenses. The club's annual turnover was now over £100,000 and the bar profits were the source of prosperity. However, when I put to him Chalky White's worry about the cost of an ambitious club like Berry Hill meeting extra travelling expenses, John said they had just bought a mini-bus: they were thinking ahead. They had had a great season: the next might even be better.

27 April

TGRD   Talking to Ray Williams, the WRU secretary, earlier in the season about the Schweppes Cup Competition, he admitted that financially at least the ideal game for the final would be Llanelli v. Cardiff. This was not meant to disparage any of the other Welsh clubs, but it is the case that these two can almost ensure that the Arms Park will be full.

And that is how it has happened this season. They represent, in the way other clubs do not, the traditional flavour of an historically special East and West Wales duel. Each club has a unique and distinctive glamour attached to it. Llanelli are blessed usually with a highly talented array of home-grown players that are the envy of other clubs. Cardiff, as the capital city club, have an air of city sophistication which, whilst it might attract players from a wider field, is a potent focus for the wrath of the provinces. People pray and long for that day of reckoning – Cardiff's come-uppance.

Both teams are proud of their reputations for producing what is best in rugby. It is a rich heritage they both possess, and a blazing charisma. Poignantly for those who have been there, particularly on the grand occasion, the unmistakable heart of Welsh rugby is at Stradey. But, or so the Cardiffian is at pains to point out, the pulse beats as strongly at their club.

This time Cardiff were the favourites. But West Walians were quick to point out who had won the Cup more times than any other club and who, if deserts were just today, would consolidate a five-win record – two more times than Cardiff. Their prayers were answered. With a final dramatic drop goal Gary Pearce won for Llanelli.

There is the eternal fascination of why we go back time and time again – the race is not always to who is believed beforehand to be the strongest and the swiftest.

10

Into Injury Time

We never do anything well till we cease to think about the manner of doing it. This is the reason why it is so difficult for any but natives to speak a language correctly and idiomatically.

William Hazlitt

JM What is striking about the season is that the team which was clearly the best of all teams, the French, did not win the Championship; while the team quite unfancied, one which delighted everybody, the Irish, did win. I thought seeing France play their matches, that there was a problem within the team hard to define. They were very gifted players. They had a clear idea of what they were doing, yet they kept on falling out among themselves or with the referee. Of course, they had the most sensational setback of the whole season when Esteve was tackled by the English scrum-half at Twickenham and lost the try when over the line. A match was drawn which they should have won. That single incident cost the Championship.

It was also true that France should have beaten Ireland in Dublin. They were scoring the tries; but the team lost its temper; forwards took against the referee. A match that should have been won was lost, the Championship was lost. Therefore, it follows that a great or good team (I won't say France were quite a *great* team) actually can lose through a temperamental element inside the team. People used to say that this was always a weakness of French teams. They were 'temperamental', as if they were some kind of mad foreigners. But we have seen the Welsh team this season give away penalty goals, behave in a silly or 'temperamental' manner that could have lost

142

them matches, perhaps did in Paris. Therefore, it is no good saying the French are not like us, that the Channel makes for different kinds of human beings. More interesting, I think, is that a team can defeat itself. I wonder if when you were playing you were aware of a team which really lost when it should have won by internal dissension or bad temper or silly behaviour?

TGRD Well, the case here is the case of France. Welsh players always say that in any game against French players there is always a moment in the match when there is this kind of argument amongst the French because things are not going the way they wish, and that is the point when you have to drive home the advantage.

But on your general point about the favourite failing, isn't that one of the fascinations of sport, one reason why we come back to play or watch week after week? It was the same in the Schweppes Cup when Llanelli pipped the favourites, Cardiff, at the post – or more accurately between them with Gary Pearce's drop.

More crucial, I think, is the fact that this year France denied their own personality. They seemed to be playing counter to their natural temperament, which has so much panache and ebullience when the players are allowed their heads. Then they are an exciting team to watch but now I think they were very much the puppets of their coach. It was Fouroux on the sideline who had determined beforehand how the French team should play. With the very talented players he had, they should have been allowed to express themselves more freely. In contrast it seemed to me, and very much against the grain of previous Irish teams, because Mick Doyle was such an understanding, generous-of-spirit coach, the Irish players were allowed to play the game as they wished and in the end proved to be successful.

JM There were many interesting Irish matches. In the

143

match with Wales, what was remarkable was that the Irish were so much more sharp, more intelligent, and that the Welsh team kept on playing into their hands. The Irish back row were very fast, yet the Welsh kept on bringing the full-back into the line to be knocked down. The Irish back row would win the ball and the Irish would be on the attack. Wales had the ball and kept on losing it. They didn't seem to realise they were keeping on losing it and that the Irish were just enjoying themselves. The Irish appraisal of the game as it was moving and developing was very striking, and extremely acute. This season the Irish joke was on the rest of the United Kingdom.

TGRD   Yes, it was a disappointment to Wales that here we were denying what we've always prided ourselves on, our ability to read the game. This year we failed to do it. The Irish, in contrast, did understand how to do just that.

JM   Looking back over the season, I think of all the important memories two of the French team stand out. One was at Twickenham when I happened to be sitting in a stand with a very unusual angle on what happened. That brilliant English wing, Underwood, was going for the corner flag. Suddenly we had this remarkable spectacle of six Frenchmen all very fast after him to stop him scoring. It was a fine sight to see these very determined tacklers going for this one man. They actually did catch him just before he scored at the corner flag. It was a very exciting angle on a match to see that happen. You grasped the speed of the play and the cover.

Another memory of the past months is Serge Blanco scoring his first try against Scotland. It had been fetching to notice at the beginning of the season in the English match the way in which the French backs seemed to be so poised and prepared. You could see them giving signals to each other. Now the scrum-half was going to give the ball very quickly to the outside-half. Blanco would move before the ball came out of the scrum. He would have run at a tremendous pace for about twenty-five yards, so that when he came between his centres, both of whom were very gifted players, it was impossible to do anything about him. In the English match it didn't work perfectly, but in the match in Paris against Scotland, he moved in exactly the same way. Of course if you watch on television you cannot grasp this expertise because at first he is out of the picture. He moved so early and so swiftly that when he actually came between the centres and he took a pass that was not intended for him, no one could stop him. He was going like the perfection of rugby football. I thought that was the high point of the season.

TGRD   In the end, what you remember about a season or any one game, are the individuals and the individual moments. Because however much coaching may demand that the line-out is right, that the scrummaging goes to plan, the memory that sticks is of the expertise, the talent and the genius of the one player. You've mentioned Blanco and I think he, as a star performer, stood out head and shoulders above everybody else this year, even including the performance of the Australian team. As far as Wales is concerned and to look for some encouragement, I think inevitably this year of someone like Mark Ring. This is what is needed in rugby football now, the return to importance of the individual player, the natural player who displays his talent.

JM   You mention Mark Ring, who had a very good season for Wales. In Paris there were two dramatic moments when Ring made brilliant breaks. In your day there would have been an outside-half or a wing three-quarter with him or a back-row forward – and he had the front-row forward alongside him. And nothing came of

it. So the individual player – and Mark Ring's performance in Paris was sparkling – has to have support still,
doesn't he?

TGRD   Of course he does. The game also needs players
who can respond to the opportunist intervention of a
team-mate. It is something that is denied to followers of
the game these days, not just in rugby, but also in soccer.
The tendency in coaching is to deny individualism. What
we need to do is put the individual back on a pedestal
once more.

JM   This season has seen the announcement of the
World Cup. Is the character of an amateur big game
going to change? Do you think the year has been one
we should regard as historic perhaps, because of the
changes that may be at hand for the rest of the century?

TGRD   Well, the International Board for once made two
very clear-cut statements during the year. From now on
they are going to allow associate membership of the
International Board, which will no longer be the exclusive club of the few countries which were once pink on the
map plus France. The game has grown enormously over
the last fifteen to twenty years, and it is important that
these other countries should be incorporated into the
International Board because they should have a say in
how the game is to develop between now and the end of
the decade.
    The Board's other announcement was, of course, their
decision to inaugurate a World Cup in 1987. That is
important, and will have an enormous effect on the game
between now and the end of the century.
    Then next year the International Board will have its
centenary year. That should be a watershed in the development of the game's administration. They will be
deciding whether they ought to have an administrative

staff to replace their present amateur set-up. If so, they will need to guard against turning into a political body which FIFA seems to have become.

JM   When you have a world-wide organisation of this kind in a game which has always, I suppose, been quite cosmopolitan but which is still an amateur game, one in which players are now going to be called upon to be brilliant and at their best, but in which they also have jobs to go to – how is it going to be feasible for players to maintain their 'standard of excellence'? They are going to be asked to travel around the world. They are going to be in a different kind of organisation, one in which they will have to be paid.

It is very possible that the Italian rugby structure will be unmasked. It may become clear that there have been intrigues or, certainly, contracts with players. Players may not be as amateur as they look to the official world. Or are players going to continue to have to do small deals? Be rewarded, while not seeming to be rewarded? Otherwise it is very difficult to see how young men, often married with children, can give so much time to a game on this new International scale.

TGRD   That is certainly a question the International Board will have to face up to. But even more important for the good health of rugby, they will need to scrap all existing arrangements for games and tours between now and the end of the decade. It isn't feasible to expect players to give up so much time to travel for their own country, as England are at the moment in New Zealand, as well as with the British Lions who go to South Africa next year, and then add on the World Cup the following year. That is far too heavy a burden for an amateur player. The World Cup should become the premier competition and all else ought to fall in line with that. As yet it seems that the list of tours that they have arranged between now and the end of the century is still in existence. I don't think it is feasible or acceptable that this World Cup should be superimposed on to what is already happening.

JM   The World Cup brings to mind the question of South Africa. Oddly enough, you and I first met in South Africa in 1968. You were playing for the Lions, I was doing some television films. One was about Nadine Gordimer and Helen Sussman and the other, which was intended as a paradigm of South African society, was about South African rugby. I talked to Danie Craven and many Afrikaner ideologues, and I presented South Africa in terms of rugby as a place that was destined for disaster. Apartheid is a bad system and I felt that going to play games in South Africa actually encouraged the system to flourish rather than, as many people quite genuinely believe, the converse.

When the Springboks came over in 1969/70 there was a riot on the ground at St. Helen's, Swansea. I remember walking on the field while it was going on and talking to a very surprised Springbok captain, their scrum-half Dawie de Villiers (later their Ambassador) whom I'd last interviewed the previous year in Cape Town. There was a magistrate's court case in Swansea later. I gave evidence for the defence of the people arrested. We won. I was very unpopular for a while at the Swansea club.

Now you have New Zealand society being torn apart in the same way because of the South African issue. The fact that legal action there has led to the cancellation of the All Blacks tour of South Africa reveals how disruptive the apartheid connection in sport can be. I read that an opinion poll showed that the majority of New Zealanders were opposed to the tour – not just other New Zealand sportsmen and women, fearful of a Commonwealth boycott for their own sport. While I sympathise with the argument that citizens in a democracy should be

148

free to travel where they wish, commonsense should suggest that when one group in society – like the NZRU or, it might be, the British Unions – offends the moral sense of a nation, a fresh element then governs the argument.

Naturally, I'm delighted that the tour is off and am impressed that the lawyers who argued for its abandonment and won an injunction are former players. The dismay in South Africa I can bear with equanimity. There are still people who believe that bridges should be built to help South Africa change. I believe the changes are still only cosmetic. Playing games will not give people of all colours equal rights. I think that the only role of South African teams in international sport is disruptive to a point that it may be better to exclude them permanently.

TGRD   Whilst I accept that apartheid in South Africa is despicable and no one in his right mind should ever accept that kind of division within society, I do take issue with you to a certain extent about whether rugby players or their Unions should make decisions based on political reasoning. It would be rather arrogant of the Rugby Union to think that by not accepting an invitation to play rugby in South Africa, it could lead to a change in the political system. And where do you draw the line? I am sure you could, if you chose, find some political reason why you shouldn't play sport in a number of countries. So once the Unions have made a decision on sporting grounds, about going to South Africa, then it's up to the individual players to discuss with their own consciences whether they want to play rugby there; and they should be allowed to do so without outside interference.

I first went to South Africa in 1968 and found it an obnoxious system, I didn't go there again until 1977, when I accepted an invitation to play rugby in Pretoria and Cape Town. After I'd made my decision I was sent a letter by a politician from the Welsh Office giving reasons why I shouldn't go. The man who wrote that letter had never been to South Africa, he'd never experienced the society there, he did not know at first hand what conditions were like and I refused to accept his suggestion, believing that I should experience things for myself, and I believe that that was the right decision to make at that time.

JM   When John Taylor the back-row forward, who was a close friend and colleague of yours in the great team, would not play against South Africa, was it felt that John was a strange man to have done such a thing? He lost a Welsh cap by doing so. He came back into the Welsh team, but was he regarded as being peculiar to have taken his stand?

TGRD   To my knowledge, he wasn't, he was still accepted, and respected for the opinions he held and the decision he made. If I could draw another example, I could understand why, for instance, the MCC has refused over many years to go to South Africa because of the Basil D'Olivera affair. It was the South Africans themselves who made the decision there and told the MCC that they would not accept Basil D'Olivera into South Africa. The MCC, quite rightly, refused to be dictated to. But that kind of situation has not yet arisen in first-class rugby.

JM   Let us suppose that a coloured or black player was picked for a British rugby team, and it could well happen in the U.K., do you think the attitudes in Britain would change because then you would be reproducing the crisis that the D'Olivera situation promoted in cricket?

TGRD   To be a man of mischief here, I would love that occasion to arise at the senior level, to see what would happen. But I suspect that nothing would because at a very junior level in the youth team a black man has already represented Wales in South Africa, Glen Webbe who now plays on the wing for Bridgend.

JM Looking at the game in the mid-eighties, it all seems to have become very technically demanding and self-conscious and earnest. Could it be that people went out more to play for fun in the old days of Haydn Tanner and Bleddyn Williams, Lewis Jones, and Ken Jones and John Gwilliam? I can remember that remarkable moment in 1953 when New Zealand were about to win and Clem Thomas suddenly kicked the ball across and Ken Jones caught it and scored a try. It looked like the sort of game we played as schoolboys. When you go now to the Arms Park, Twickenham or the Parc des Princes, people look as if they are playing in a different intellectual climate. Players are not running out there for a bit of fun. They clearly have their national destinies in their hands. I'd like to say to them, let's not have to work things out as if we are Napoleon at the Battle of Austerlitz, wishing to transform the history of warfare.

More simply, teams, or their Unions, should be more in touch with the spirit of the crowd. Or has the crowd itself become infected by the spirit of management and the coach? If so, I am not a part of the crowd any more. I belong to a crowd that's gone. Surely the crowd has much more even now of the desire for delight in it than the people who are in charge comprehend? I would like to think that was true.

TGRD I think it *is* true. As a spectator these days I'm even more aware of it, that the people who watch the game want that sense of joy, the sense of delight and spontaneity in a team. The crowd live their game through the players and a couple of years ago, when Wales were not playing well, and winning games perhaps marginally through penalties, there was a sense

151

of quietness, disappointment afterwards, and no joy in the discussion. I quite agree with you that what the coaches demand of the game is not necessarily what the spectators demand of the game. They come to see some excitement, to see genius at play and, to come back to the point we made earlier, they want to see the genius and the talent of the individual player. The game as it is played at the moment gives little satisfaction to the people who follow it.

JM When you now, writing for *The Times*, watch England play or Scotland or Ireland or France or New Zealand or Australia, do you have a strong sense of nationality? Do you feel a distance from the way in which these other countries play? I find it quite strange, going to watch all these other countries and talking to English and Scottish and French rugby players. I always have a feeling that their rugby is not our rugby. This is a very unfair judgement, an absurd thing to say, but they don't look at rugby as we understand it. It's daft for me to think that but for you, perhaps, it's different, because you played against these people in Internationals for so many years. Do you see them as different kinds of rugby players from the Welsh?

TGRD Whenever Cardiff played the Harlequins on an Easter Monday, I was never more aware of the physical difference between Englishmen and Welshmen than at that moment. The London Harlequins always seemed huge, much taller, much longer in the leg than us. But if you went by appearance you would never win any games. So it must have been a case of applying native cunning and Welsh rugby-playing intuition to win the day in the end.

But on an International level, different nations have different perceptions. New Zealanders, for example, appreciate their back rows. It is the flankers, the No. 8, occasionally their locks, who are the heroes in New Zealand. In Wales our heroes are at half-back or in the centre or at full-back. In South Africa and in New Zealand the tendency is to organisation and discipline. It's a grimmer approach, possibly, that thinks in terms of groups of players. Whereas in Wales we may look back in history and remember the terrible eight at the beginning of the century, but mostly we salute the individual genius – we remember Mervyn Davies and John Taylor, Gareth Edwards and Barry John and Phil Bennett. And it is the flowering of the individual player that we need to see again in Wales.

JM   My weakness, I think, has always been to see life as a game. The pleasure of the last season is to recognise that there is a game that is a life.

Appendix I
The Five Nations Championship 1985

2 February
SCOTLAND v. IRELAND   15-18
Scorers   *Scotland*:   Dods – 4P; Robertson – 1DG
   Ireland: Ringland – 2T; Kiernan – 1P, 1DG, 2C

2 February
ENGLAND v. FRANCE   9-9
Scorers   *England*:   Andrew – 1DG, 2P
   France: Lescarboura – 3DG

16 February
FRANCE v. SCOTLAND   11-3
Scorers   *France*:   Blanco – 2T; Lescarboura – 1P
   Scotland: Dods – 1P

2 March
IRELAND v. FRANCE   15-15
Scorers   *Ireland*:   Kiernan – 5P
   France: Estève – 1T; Cordorniou – 1T;
   Lescarboura – 2C, 1P

2 March
SCOTLAND v. WALES   21-25
Scorers   *Scotland*:   Paxton – 2T; Rutherford – 2DG;
   Dods – 2C, 1P
   Wales: Pickering – 2T; Davies – 1DG;
   Wyatt – 1C, 4P

16 March
WALES v. IRELAND   9-21
Scorers   *Wales*:   Lewis – 1T; Davies – 1DG; Wyatt – 1C
          Ireland: Ringland – 1T; Crossan – 1T;
                       Kiernan – 2C, 3P

16 March
ENGLAND v. SCOTLAND   10-7
Scorers   *England*:   Smith – 1T; Andrew – 2P
          Scotland: Robertson – 1T; Dods – 1P

30 March
IRELAND v. ENGLAND   13-10
Scorers   *Ireland*:   Mullin – 1T; Kiernan – 1DG, 2P
          England: Underwood – 1T; Andrew – 2P

30 March
FRANCE v. WALES   14-3
Scorers   *France*:   Estève – 1T; Gallion – 1T;
                       Lescarboura – 2P
          Wales: Thorburn – 1P

20 April
WALES v. ENGLAND   24-15
Scorers   *Wales*:   Roberts – 1T; Davies – 1T, 1DG;
                       Thorburn – 2C, 3P
          England: Smith – 1T; Andrew – 2P, 1C, 1DG

FINAL CHAMPIONSHIP TABLE

	P	W	D	L	F	A	Pts
IRELAND	4	3	1	0	67	49	7
FRANCE	4	2	2	0	49	30	6
WALES	4	2	0	2	61	71	4
ENGLAND	4	1	1	2	44	53	3
SCOTLAND	4	0	0	4	46	64	0

Appendix II

Welsh Rugby Union
Schweppes Cup Final

17 November   First Round

Tonyrefail v. Cardiff   Newport Saracens v. Llanelli
9-22   9-19

19 December   Second Round

Bryncoch v. Cardiff   Risca v. Llanelli
0-21   12-52

26 January   Third Round

Newbridge v. Cardiff   Llandovery v. Llanelli
6-24   4-42

23 February   Fourth round

Cardiff v. Neath   Llanelli v. South Wales Police
21-12   23-13

23 March   Semi-Final

Cardiff v. Pontypool   Llanelli v. Bridgend
24-3   24-10

27 April   Final

CARDIFF   v.   LLANELLI
14-15

Appendix III

John Player Cup 1984–85

First Round	Second Round	Third Round	Fourth Round	Quarter-Finals	Semi-Finals	FINAL
Maidenhead (3) v. O. Redcliffians (9)	Sidcup (24) v. O. Redcliffians (7)	Bath (24) v. Berry Hill (3)	Bath (37) v. Blackheath (3)	Sale (15) v. Bath (25)	Gloucester (11)	
Devon/Cornwall Police (4) v. Lydney (15)	Oxford OB (12) v. Lydney (21)	Wakefield (6) v. Blackheath (6)			v.	
Hendon (15) v. Crawley (18)	Redruth (14) v. Crawley (4)	Sale (33) v. Aspatria (10)	Lydney (4) v. Sale (20)		Bath (12)	
Oxford OB (13) v. Swindon (12)		Redruth (11) v. Lydney (29)				BATH beat LONDON WELSH 24-15
Barker's Butts (10) v. Bromsgrove (9)	Bedford (10) v. Barker's Butts (4)	Gloucester (29) v. Richmond (0)	Gloucester (29) v. Saracens (3)	Gloucester (31)		
Redruth (26) v. Bletchley (9)	Hartlepool R (10) v. Aspatria (16)	Saracens (16) v. Gosforth (13)		v.		
Preston G'hoppers (9) v. H'pool R. (9)	Nuneaton (13) v. Wakefield (17)	Harlequins (29) v. Ealing (12)	Harlequins (16) v. Lichfield (6)	Harlequins (12)		
Alnwick (9) v. Wakefield (34)	Lichfield (17) v. Stourbridge (10)	Lichfield (11) v. Sidcup (4)				
Lichfield (21) v. Loughboro' S. (3)		Headingley (10) v. London Welsh (18)	Nottingham (11) v. London Welsh (12)	London Welsh (21)	Coventry (10)	
Bedford (51) v. Rushden/Higham (0)	Blackheath (40) v. Sutton & Epsom (6)	Nottingham (15) v. Northampton (3)		v.	v.	
Aspatria (19) v. B'head Pk. (7)		Bedford (6) v. Waterloo (7)	Waterloo (21) v. Wasps (13)	Waterloo (0)		
Nuneaton (16) v. Paviors (14)	Havant (7) v. Berry Hill (27)	Wasps (23) v. Rosslyn Park (10)				
Havant (24) v. KCS OB (11)		Plymouth Albion (6) v. Coventry (42)	Moseley (9) v. Coventry (29)	Coventry (10) (winners on tries)	London Welsh (10) (winner on tries)	
Fullerians (9) v. Rosslyn Park (29)	Rosslyn Park (15) v. North Walsham (7)	West Hartlepool (9) v. Moseley (12)		v.		
Sidcup (19) v. Ipswich (6)		Leicester (43) v. Bristol (4)	Liverpool (9) v. Leicester (37)	Leicester (10)		
		Liverpool (16) v. London Scottish (13)				